LONDON'S UNDERGROUND

LONDON'S UNDERGROUND

H. F. HOWSON

LONDON

IAN ALLAN LTD

First published 1951
This edition 1986
Reprinted 1988

ISBN 0 7110 1559 7

© Ian Allan Ltd 1986

Published by Ian Allan Ltd,
Shepperton, Surrey; and printed
by Ian Allan Printing Ltd at their
works at Coombelands in
Runnymede, England

Front cover:
A train formed of 1972 Mk 1
stock is seen at East Finchley.
John Glover

Rear cover, top:
A six-car train of 1938 tube stock
arrives at Kingsbury on the
Stanmore branch of the
Metropolitan, now the Jubilee
Line. *John Glover*

Rear cover, bottom:
A line up of service stock at
Acton Works shows (from left to
right) Surface Pilot Motors
L126/7, Tube Pilot Motors L134/5
and Sleet Locomotive ESL107.
John Glover

Right:
In Leinster Gardens, Bayswater,
false fronted houses were
constructed over the railway,
which ran beneath at right
angles. They remain today, a
facade between two hotels.
John Glover

Contents

Overleaf:
City workers join a train of
C stock on a Circle Line working
via Victoria at Mansion House.
Commuting is one of the major
businesses of the Underground.
John Glover

Introduction

In the 35 years since this book was first published, great changes have taken place on the Underground system. Indeed, this introduction was being written when London Regional Transport, the present parent body of the Underground, was barely a year old. But in terms of the environment in which it operates, what in 1951 was together with the trams, trolleybuses and diesel buses the universal provider of passenger transport, London's public transport now has to cope with two million private cars licensed in the Greater London area.

The role of the Underground has thus changed. More attractive to passengers than the bus, the railway system of today caters for three main types of journey. These are the suburb to centre commuter flows and other radial trips (40%), the local journeys made wholly within the central area (also 40%), and other trips (20%). It is the daily surges of commuters who bring with them the major problems. The system is geared to provide a service for them, but the assets of infrastructure, equipment and staff then tend to be under-employed during off-peak hours. But the reward of an effective public transport system is to relieve streets that would otherwise suffer acute traffic congestion, and bringing social and economic benefits to the communities served. Urban railways are thus deemed generally to merit public moneys to pay for their construction, and as a rule continuing subsidies towards operational costs not met from fares.

It was not always so, as this book shows. The frenzied activity in Underground railway construction between 1863 when the first part of the Metropolitan Line opened, and the completion of the last central London tube line for 60 years in 1906 was as a result of private capital being employed for private gain — even if the profits turned out to be rather less than anticipated. After 1906, lines were extended into the country and to what consequently became the suburbs, tunnels were enlarged, and station platforms lengthened. Improved methods of handling traffic long predated the traffic management expertise of the highway engineer of recent years. But these measures could not keep pace with traffic growth indefinitely, and the opening of the Victoria Line in stages between 1968 and 1971 was a belated recognition of the inadequacies of some of the links in the network then in existence.

Coincident with the physical development of the system was the pursuit of technical excellence. The trains became more sophisticated, with greater space being available for passengers rather than equipment, whilst the coming of the air-operated door dispensed with the need for gatemen to be stationed at the ends of the cars. At stations, the escalator replaced lifts. Technology assisted the development of control systems, whilst on the track, signalling systems were perfected and the welding of rails did much to reduce rail wear. Ticket machines enabled passengers to serve themselves long before the checkout became commonplace in the retail trade. Good industrial design became the hallmark of the system, epitomised by the roundel. This was recently described in a national newspaper as 'neither a poke in the eye, nor a visual excitement, but is an old friend, a simple and plain spoken character. . . As a design it has an honest simplicity. The circle is evocative of wheel and place, the bar is a practical vehicle for name and designation. Everybody knows what it signifies, recognises what it represents, reacts to what it implies. TOP MARKS'.

Despite the great age of much of the system, most of it has been modernised to cope with current conditions. The scene is Embankment station on a summer day with London full of overseas visitors. The west-bound platform is crowded. A train comes in (D78, smooth and powerful). Its 24 doors slide open and in less than a minute the crowd has been ingested. But already more people arrive and a following train is on the indicator. There can hardly be a more animate scene anywhere, unless it is on the tube at Oxford Circus during the rush hour.

As the reader will find in the following pages, this is essentially a physical record of the Underground's development, concentrating on the growth of a vast system of electrified lines from a short stretch of smoky steam railway. It is a remarkable story of achievement, and one which the author hopes has provided material for an interesting book. But an organisation is only as good as its staff. The 22,000 people employed on the Underground range from signal engineers to timetable compilers, from welders to drivers, and countless others applying their hard-learned skills to the job in hand — and not forgetting the canteen ladies, playing their essential role. No one can be left out. Collectively, they are indirectly accountable to millions of ordinary people — commuters, housewives, schoolchildren — to keep this vast and complex system functioning safely and efficiently, day in and endlessly day out. Their combined efforts contribute to what, in the writer's opinion, and hopefully the reader's, is a success story.

Acknowledgements
From the first, the author realised then that in attempting to write comprehensively about London's underground railways he would need to consult many records and visit most of the places mentioned in the book. This was accomplished only by the helpful courtesy of officials of the (then)

London Transport Executive, and others not directly concerned with the Executive.

Again, when revising each of the earlier books, the author was quickly made aware that courtesy and help were forthcoming in the same generous manner. Also to those who kindly made provision for the author to visit their various departments — and to all other people concerned who may read this, whether they are still in harness or retired — he extends his thanks, and blesses the spirit of comradeship peculiar to railway folk that made his task enjoyable.

Right:
The experimental installation at Vauxhall, where the prototypes for the Underground Ticketing System (UTS) were tried out. *John Glover*

Below:
Dot matrix indicators are now telling passengers how long they have to wait as well as the destination of the next train. This view is of the northbound platform of the Northern Line at Charing Cross. *John Glover*

1
Two Historic Railways

On 16 May 1963, London celebrated the centenary of the birth of its underground railway system. A gathering of invited transport officials from various parts of the world was shown the modern Underground system at work and in contrast, part of its history in review. The spectacle included a replica of the very earliest train complete with passengers in the period dress, and a parade of steam and electric rolling stock spanning 100 years of operation.

This was the beginning, the culmination of ideas born earlier, in the days when gentlemen wore stove-pipe hats, and ladies wore crinolines; when some person thought of trains that would start in London's suburbs, and then plunge beneath the City's buildings and streets to disgorge passengers in its very centre — or even to take them right under London to the other side. At about this time a trip to the moon by aerial machine was also being considered, but the overriding opinion of city gentlemen was that neither of the ideas was worth a second thought.

Knowing what we do about railways today, it is difficult for us to imagine the scepticism of people in those far-off days. They heard about the scheme to run a railway under London, and it seemed fantastic. They ridiculed it — not only those uneducated, but also some whom today we should regard as level-headed and clear-thinking. Perhaps their attitude was not unreasonable, for only 20 years before the Underground idea was broached, London had no railway at all. In 1836 the first line began to work between Spa Road and Deptford, and it is legitimate to suppose that 20 years later many Londoners had never even travelled on a train.

They walked, for the most part, or, if obliged to travel far afield, went on horseback or took hackney carriages or seats on the new-type horse-bus, whose speed in London was not much more than six miles an hour. Their idea of a tunnel was probably something wet, dark and slimy; and contemporary pictures of the trains of their times suggest a reason why Londoners were chary of being drawn through 'sewers', as they called them, behind steam- and smoke-erupting locomotives.

Such was the unpromising birth of an early-Victorian idea which has developed into our own safe and efficient Underground, where trains may and do safely follow one another so closely as to leave only a few seconds between the departure of one and arrival of the next. We have reached the stage where almost nothing can surprise us, and if anybody ventures a suggestion of 100mph deep level tubes in the future, we merely nod and say, 'Yes, that is what it will come to one day, I suppose'.

For London's first underground railway was have to thank Charles Pearson, City solicitor, who suggested it to 'relieve the congestion of London's streets'. That sounds rather odd to us today, who imagine, not without a certain local pride, perhaps, that traffic problems are exclusive to our own age. Nevertheless, there it was, even in those days when underground railways were only an idea in the brain of Mr Pearson, and he was holding meeting after meeting trying to convince Londoners that his scheme was workable and would solve the street traffic problem. London was then comfortably full of its own citizens, and in addition was having to absorb many thousands of visitors who wanted to enjoy a novel rail journey on the new lines into town, and it appears that many of them must have taken single tickets and settled there, thus adding to the congestion!

It is estimated that at that time (c1850) over 750,000 people entered London every day, either by main line railways or by road, and the streets were becoming blocked by a great variety of iron-tyred vehicles — omnibuses, coaches, hackney carriages, drays, and so forth — all making a vast din on the cobbled roads. With frayed nerves and tempers Londoners looked around for alleviation, and the Press found a very nice topic in the 'scandalous state of London's transport facilities', at the same time affording space for comment on grandiose schemes for relieving the streets of much of their traffic. One such scheme was for the construction of a wide street, roofed over with glass, which would encircle the Metropolis and would have beneath it no fewer than four double lines of railway. A magnificent project this, and had it been carried out (without the glass roofing) it would perhaps have been all the better for modern London.

None of these schemes was adopted — unless one could regard Pearson's plan as a drastically curtailed version of the project just described. To him is attributed a scheme for an underground railway between Farringdon Street and Bishops' Road, Paddington, although it seems probable that this was an elaboration of an original idea of his for a shorter line. At all events, with the help of Stevens, Architect and Surveyor to the City (Western Division), a plan was eventually evolved for an underground, steam-operated railway nearly four miles long between Farringdon Street and Bishop's Road, Paddington, following Farringdon Road and King's Cross Road to King's Cross, and then more or less beneath the course of Euston Road, Marylebone Road and Praed Street to Paddington. Thus it would serve as a link between three main-line railway termini — the Great Western at Paddington, the London & North Western at Euston, and the Great Northern at King's Cross. It was, in fact, destined to serve a major newcomer as well — the Midland, which at first used King's Cross station as its Metropolitan terminal, commencing a passenger service between there and Hitchin, where a branch line to Bedford linked it to the Midland Counties in 1858.

Farringdon Street was chosen as a site for the eastern terminus principally because the City Cattle Market, then occupying the site, was about to be moved to the Caledonian Road at Islington.* The Act of Parliament obtained by the North Metropolitan Railway Company in 1853, however, authorised only the construction of a railway between Edgware Road and Battle Bridge (King's Cross) and it was necessary to obtain further powers by new Acts in order to extend the line to the points mentioned.

The constructional work began in 1860, and within 2½ years it was completed, a remarkable achievement considering the amount of work involved in diverting sewers and gas and water mains, with very little in the way of previous experience to guide the constructors in their task.

It was at first suggested by Fowler, the North Metropolitan Railway Company's engineer, that trains for the new underground railway might be successfully run on the compressed air principle. They would be 'blown through' the tunnels by compressed air generated in great compressors at each end of the line, and if fact a narrow gauge railway of this type materialised in London in 1863, for conveying parcels underground from the North Western Post Office in Seymour Street to the London Chief Post Office in the City. The freight of this odd line was carried in trucks to which was attached a shield, or piston, flanged with rubber and fitting snugly to the tunnel walls. The trains were sucked or blown backwards or forwards by air under pressure, but success was short-lived because the compressed air leaked continuously through the tunnel joints.†

This possibility may have been already foreseen when Fowler proposed his compressed air traction and in any case the idea was abandoned, in favour of steam propulsion employing locomotives constructed without a firebox, so as to avoid the pollution of tunnels by smoke from normally fired locomotives. The fireless locomotive was to have had a plain cylindrical boiler charged with hot water and steam under pressure, and experiment had shown that if it were re-charged at each end of the line, the loss of pressure on such a short journey would be slight, even after making full allowance for stopping and restarting. A large firebrick heater on the locomotive would have assisted in maintaining the necessary pressure, but this idea was abandoned, too, and the underground railway started work with locomotives of orthodox type, the smoke problem being left for solution in the light of running experience.

The Metropolitan Railway, as it became known, was built on the 'cut and cover' method. Where it was to run under streets a huge trench was dug, lined with brickwork and roofed over, and the streets relaid for surface traffic.

---

*It became a famous market there, but latterly dealt with things other than cattle.
†Parts of this old tunnel still exist and are used by British Telecom as telephone ducts.

12

Although this method of construction made chasms of certain streets and must have paralysed traffic in their immediate vicinity, it made possible the construction of the line without interfering to any great extent with private property. By all accounts there was not much interference, although owners of property along the route were not slow in claiming for structural defects which, they averred, were indirectly caused by 'digging an enormous ditch' in front of their property. Some idea of the amount of earth or 'spoil' excavated for that early railway can be gathered by those who know the Chelsea football ground at Stamford Bridge. The terraces there were raised from that spoil.

The job of constructing such a railway would be deemed an intricate one even today; but it was done successfully — and substantially, be it added, for the original massive brickwork is still in good condition. The only real setback occurred when the Fleet Ditch Sewer burst and flooded the workings to a depth of 10ft as far as King's Cross, but even this proved only a temporary check.

One can well imagine Londoners of that period taking a keen interest in the progress of their railway. In that robust infancy of photographic recording, some of the works were under camera fire, and these pictures have fortunately been preserved, forming a remarkable retrospect of a London that is now beyond living memory. To the Londoner of the 1860s, the work was one of vast proportions, which ripped open many of his familiar streets, creating upheaval on a scale incredible and impossible to our modern age; besides it was unique, daring and a portent of thrills to come. The latter were reserved on Private View Day for Mr and Mrs Gladstone and other notables who rode through the echoing tunnels, and were photographed, in open trucks. Then to celebrate the opening of the railway many hundreds of people were invited to attend a great banquet at Farringdon Street Station — and the trains, as they approached the station, were heralded by music from a band!

The fortunate Londoner who secured a seat on the trains on that day of public running, 10 January 1863, must have experienced thrills forever memorable. Incidentally, the public rode in closed carriages; it was only on the first trial trips that open trucks were used. The original section of the Metropolitan tracks was laid to a mixed gauge (standard and GW 7ft), and at first the GW supplied the motive power, rolling stock and personnel. But, apparently outraged at not receiving an allotment of shares in the Moorgate Street extension, the GW gave the Metropolitan six months' notice of its intention to quit. If fact, the GW withdrew all the material at such short notice that the Metropolitan had to call for help on the GN, who, no doubt elated at the disappearance of broad gauge interests, handsomely responded. The GW quit on 11 August 1863, and next morning Londoners found the Metropolitan running with makeshift stock and a scratch crew, hastily mustered. Six trains came to grief by derailment that day, but the Metropolitan soon had order restored, and on 1 October took delivery of its new carriages, which were finished externally in varnished teak, the 'firsts' being painted white above the waist as a distinction. That was the end of Brunel's 7ft gauge underground, and by 1873 the broad gauge rails had finally disappeared.

It was foreseen at the outset that the Metropolitan would eventually connect with other railway systems, and subsequently this occurred; the Great Western operated a service from Windsor to Farringdon Street via a junction at Paddington; the Midland, Great Northern and Great Eastern Railways connected through underground junctions at King's Cross and Liverpool Street respectively, and the London, Chatham & Dover Railway was linked at Farringdon Street by a short connecting line from Blackfriars.

Londoners took to their railway with open arms and purses, as witness that 9,500,000 people were carried the first year, 12,000,000 the second, and each year thereafter more and more came. It was a triumph for the much criticised and mistakenly dubbed 'sewer' railway, whose popularity was further enhanced by the addition of two trains exclusively for workmen. One ran to the City in the early morning and the other ran from the City in the evening, carrying bona fide workmen for a fare of one penny (1d) for each single journey.

The Metropolitan was run almost exclusively as a passenger railway, although that was not the original intention, since we read that the City of London Corporation subscribed £200,000 towards its construction, believing that the Metropolitan would clear the City streets of a considerable amount of goods traffic. Perhaps it did serve that purpose in a roundabout way by decreasing the number of omnibuses, or at least by limiting their increase. There may be some who, remembering the old Metropolitan Railway in its steam days would also remember its contemporary, the District Railway. This line was built to serve an area of West London whose inhabitants having been made rail-conscious by the advent of the Metropolitan, were looking forward to the day when they, too, would be connected to the City by rail.

The Metropolitan in its early days catered only for people wishing to travel between the northern boundaries of the City and Paddington; in fact it served merely the fringes of Central London. This fact did not long escape the notice of railway financiers who also noted that the busiest surface routes were *across* the capital, from east to west. Regular travellers on these routes were simply crying out for an underground railway, and it was rightly judged that they would patronise it to a greater extent than the Metropolitan. Thus, the second underground railway in London, and in the world for that matter, was born and named the Metropolitan District Railway.

The 'Twin Lines' as they have been referred to, were both murky, sulphurous and extremely grimy compared with today's Underground, but in the 1860s that was a matter of little account. They provided a means of travel much faster than anything along the streets, and those streets were incredibly slushy at times; at least it was warm and dry below ground.

The histories of the 'Twin Lines' are so intermingled that one cannot very well refer to the one without the other. A few years after the opening of the Metropolitan, the District came into operation, and thereafter each line carried out a programme of extension with the same object in view — to bring the suburbs and the underdeveloped country beyond into direct rail communication with Central London.

The first section of the District Railway was opened late in the year 1868 between South Kensington and Westminster, a distance of just over two miles. For its first 2½ years it was worked by Metropolitan stock, under an agreement between the two companies, but in the meantime it had extended its lines eastward under Victoria Embankment to Blackfriars. In fact, the Embankment and the District line extension were built together, but the railway was opened first — in May 1870, preceding the roadway by some six weeks.

In the meantime, extension westward was contemplated. Kensington lay in the Western outskirts, and beyond was practically open country, with places like Hammersmith and Chiswick still villages but rapidly growing. The population of Greater London was then nearly four millions, and such was the demand for transport, partly from residents on the outskirts who wanted to 'see the shops', that an extension of the line westwards into the country was regarded as essential, and justifiable as a good long-term financial proposition.

The Metropolitan had meanwhile been driving steadily east and west, its plan appearing roughly in the shape of an inverted 'U', with the ends curving towards the river Thames. In the west a railway between Hammersmith Broadway and Bishops Road (Paddington) was opened as an extension of the Metropolitan, and in the east Moorgate Street was soon reached.* There was also a service to Addison Road, Kensington (now Olympia), over a spur opened in 1864 from Latimer Road, on the Hammersmith-Bishops Road line, to the West London Railway. This service was worked by a stock detached from Hammersmith trains, and ultimately gave a direct connection to the District at Earls Court. As from February 1872, this route became part of the 'Outer Circle', which was worked by the LNWR between Mansion House and Broad Street, via Addison Road and Willesden.

Then from Baker Street the Metropolitan branched out northwest to Swiss Cottage, over what was known as the St John's Wood Railway — and also at that time the first train ran on the new Aylesbury & Buckingham Railway. The promoters of the latter line could scarcely have imagined that their railway, remote and unconnected with the London Underground system as it was then, would ever become part of the distant and greater whole.

Nevertheless, it is a fact that Sir Edward Watkin, Chairman of the Metropolitan Railway from 1872 to 1894, had a much greater scheme than

---

*The 'street' was dropped by the civic authority early in the 20th century, but the present station still displayed at least one board with the older title until well after World War II.

this in mind when he envisaged the Metropolitan as part of a great trunk railway from the Midlands and the North across London to Dover and thence to the Continent via the Channel Tunnel. This bold concept, worthy of so redoubtable a prospector, who also directed the destinies of other railways directly concerned, was only partly realised. With Metropolitan assistance, the new trunk line — the Great Central, a renamed and enlarged Manchester, Sheffield & Lincolnshire Railway — reached London, and possibly our own future may reveal that a trunk railway from the Midlands projected southwards to the Continent of Europe was not fantastic but merely premature.

But although he failed to obtain support for his greater plan, Sir Edward at least had the satisfaction of seeing the glorious country north-west of London brought within easy access of the City by rail. Metroland, as it became known, was made available to Londoners to live in and to explore on foot by the extension of the Metropolitan Railway to Chesham and ultimately to Aylesbury, which was reached by the absorption of an independent and isolated undertaking, the Aylesbury & Buckingham Railway previously mentioned.

In the east, too, the Metropolitan had been busy tunnelling under the City streets towards Aldgate. The purpose behind these short and enormously expensive City extensions was eventually to link the Metropolitan with the District, and so form the Inner Circle line, over which both railways intended to run services to their mutual benefit.

To effect this most important link each company agreed to build part of the City Lines & Extension Railway, by which name the connecting line was to be known. Its length was but 1mile 10chains, connecting at a junction with the District at Mansion House, running thence due east to Mark Lane and finally curving north to make a junction with the Metropolitan at Aldgate station. It involved considerable demolition work on the surface as well as street reconstruction in the neighbourhood of the Tower, but by its completion in 1884 an Inner Circle line, already made continuous in the west by a junction at South Kensington, became an accomplished fact. London Transport designates this the Circle Line.

The Twin Lines system also connected in that year with the East London Railway, a 4½-mile extending from Shoreditch to New Cross, where it forked to serve respectively the South Eastern and the London, Brighton & South Coast stations. This new link enabled through trains to be run between Hammersmith and New Cross via a spur tunnel at Whitechapel and the Thames Tunnel, of which more later.

This period in the growth of railways can be likened on a smaller geographical scale to the present air age, when hundreds of towns all over the world have, within a few years, built themselves air terminals and taken their places on main and feeder air routes. The District in its steam days also built up a very extensive suburban system, thrusting out lines to Harrow, Ealing

16

and Hounslow through undeveloped country, in the certainty that population would follow wherever the rail penetrated. Its services reached Richmond and Wimbledon in the south west, and East Ham, Barking, and ultimately Upminster in the east, although the latter came long after electrification. In view of a Working Party Report, referred to later, to link various Southern Region suburban lines by a new 'tube' it is interesting that as far back as 1881 a 7½-mile line was projected to connect Surbiton, on the London & South Western main line, with Putney Bridge on the District's Fulham extension. This link was never constructed, and instead the LSWR built a line from Putney to Wimbledon and granted the District running powers over it.

To prolong the subject of the growth of the Twin Lines system, however, is to risk passing unconsciously from the steam to the electric era. So far, all these miles of railway in and around London were steam operated. Electric traction cuts cleanly across the story, leaving its predecessor completely outdated, although the steam-worked underground in its time had proved a real blessing by conveying our great-grandparents swiftly and cheaply into and about London, offering unheard-of facilities for glorious shopping expeditions, and excursions to the cleaner outer suburbs, where ultimately many casual patrons settled and became season-ticket holders.

So if only for the sake of rounding off the story of the two pioneer underground steam railways, honourable mention must be made of the trains and the services they ran so faithfully during their 40-odd years of steam traction.

The steam locomotives of both the Metropolitan and the District railways were expressions of a single design that conferred on the Twin Lines an obvious and striking similarity. These engines were 4-4-0Ts built by Beyer, Peacock & Company to a stock type that became widely known and admired, and, as was to be expected from so eminent a firm, they were handsome, sturdy and efficient. Also, they were longlasting, as witness that all the locomotives supplied to the District from 1871 to 1905, 44 in all, were said to be still in traffic in the latter year, when electrification was accomplished. Their olive green colour combined with polished brass dome covers gave the locomotives a smart appearance it was said, even though they operated in smoke-laden tunnels.

In one particular, they were uncommon for the period, in that they were fitted with condensing gear, which gave the driver a means of diverting exhaust steam from the chimney outlet into the water tanks, where the exhaust condensed, leaving the tunnels more or less clear of smoke and vapour. In return, of course, the blast on the fire was considerably reduced and the power of the engine correspondingly impaired, whereas to maintain schedules between stations so close together needed a pretty lively engine. By rule the driver would operate his 'condensing' lever on approaching a tunnel section, and restore the chimney exhaust wherever the line was not enclosed, but from the sulphurous state of the tunnels, which not a few passengers found actively nauseating, it seems that many men only partly observed the golden rule, or not at all, for the sake of timekeeping. There was, however, a ready-made excuse; after a time, the water in the tanks grew so hot that steam would no longer condense.

The original passenger coaches were divided into first, second and third class compartments, the first class being fitted with carpets, mirrors and well-upholstered seats. No doubt they offset to some extent the discomfort caused by penetrating smoke in such confined spaces. Furnishings decreased in elegance according to the class, as did the space allotted per person, and we can imagine that the third class passenger was usually glad to re-surface, somewhere stiff after a ride during which all the windows had to be kept closed. It seems a little incongruous in view of this that there should have been a 'No Smoking' rule, impartially applied to all classes.

Carriage lighting was, of course, a matter of importance, and both oil and gas lamps are reported as in use at first on the Metropolitan. With a certain grim fascination and perhaps doubtful acceptance we read of suspended oil lamps that dripped and whiffed for little better purpose than making the darkness visible, so passengers wishing to read bought candles and stuck them on the window ledges, giving the compartment a most homely atmosphere. There are, however, reliable reports that gas was used at an early date,* and in this respect the Metropolitan pioneered in a way that now arouses interest.

For some years, coal gas was carried in long indiarubber bags housed in a sort of clerestory or 'tunnel' on top of the carriage roofs, but in 1878 the District improved on this method of lighting by substituting oil gas compressed into wrought-iron cylinders hung below the carriage. The gas was produced at Lillie Bridge Depot and transported at night in mobile containers to various points on the system, where the carriage cylinders could be recharged. The use of compressed oil-gas afterwards spread throughout the country.

An interesting device on steam trains in their later years was the 'next station indicator', introduced in 1894; a premonitory gadget fixed on the roof inside each compartment. The indicator was operated either by the guard, who pulled a cord bringing into view a tablet with the name of the next station, or automatically by a treadle on the track which tripped a lever on the engine. One can imagine that both methods were unreliable, especially if the guard forgot, and, at all events, the indicators did not become a permanent feature.

Of the signalling system used on these railways, the few comments that would be of interest now concern the Metropolitan at a very early date. On the single-track stretch between Baker Street and Swiss cottage some security

---

*It appeared that the Metropolitan used gas in its first coaches, delivered October 1863, and possibly the oil pots refer to a somewhat later date when the L&NW trains began to work over the system.

against head-on collisions was essential, and at that time the up and down trains crossed at St Johns Wood, where a passing loop existed. So a pilotman was appointed to accompany each train in turn over the single-line south of the loop, and another was similarly allotted to each train on the single track north thereof; to avoid misundertanding, one wore a red cap and the other's cap was blue. Hence the presence of the proper pilotman at either end of either bottleneck guaranteed the driver a safe conduct. St Johns Wood soon became a noted place for acrobatics, because here each man changed over to the other's train, which he had to pilot to his original starting point, and the seconds counted. On drawing level with the train waiting at the opposite platform face, the incoming pilotman would nimbly leap off the moving engine and join the outgoing footplate in a swift and sure-footed hop, skip and jump across the platform.

This 'human token' system lasted only a short time before it gave way to the similar but less spectacular one of a wooden 'single-line' staff carried by the guard. At one time there was also a system of signal flags is use at the junction at Baker Street. There, in a dimly-lit recess, a signalman passed his working hours in thrusting flags through certain holes so as to give the drivers visible warning or reassurance as to the state of the line ahead. One feels, however, that this method of signalling was in the nature of improvisation, since the block system of signalling was in use for many years before automatic signalling came to supersede it.

One of the biggest problems confronting the engineers of the underground steam railways was to provide and maintain a supply of breathable air in tunnels and stations. The Metropolitan engines burned coke, which is clean but gives off poisonous fumes, and after abortive trials with additional ventilators at the stations, the railway went over to coal, with the immediate result of an extremely smoky atmosphere. As a remedy, certain openings originally provided in the covered way at King's Cross and elsewhere for lighting purposes were adapted as smoke vents, and finally 'blow holes' were bored all along the route between King's Cross and Edgware Road. They were covered by gratings in the roadways above, and were prone to sudden belching of steamy vapour which startled the passing horses.

Bearing the smoke problem in mind, the later District Railway engineers built their line in open cutting wherever possible and avoided much of the nuisance. This was not possible along the Embankment and City sections, and here ventilators proved essential and unduly costly because of the need for camouflage. In the neighbourhood of Temple Gardens all surface evidences of an underground railway were frowned upon, excepting Temple Station itself, and the pump house chimney stack there had to be carried horizontally right along the station wall, and up the side of a neighbouring building, where it was decently screened by the wall and could smoke without giving offence.

It was perhaps in the nature of things that the fortunes of these two railways should fluctuate, for so much about them was purely trial and error, and experiments cost money, although often unsuccessful. The District Railway in particular had many lean years, but curiously enough its prospects were brightened by events that its promoters could hardly have foreseen. These were the exhibitions held annually at South Kensington, and followed by the famous exhibitions at Earls Court. The great American and Buffalo Bill show there in 1887 was immensely popular, and even more so was the Universal Exhibition of nine years later, when the big Wheel made its debut and provided thrills which attracted thousands of Londoners and visitors from all over the country. The District Railway took full advantage of these displays and issued combined rail and entry tickets.

There must at one time have been hundreds of interestingly human stories in circulation that had as a background the underground steam railways of London, but not many survive. Two which have been handed down, perhaps losing accuracy in the process, serve to illustrate the leisurely nature of rail travel in those bygone days. It is said that a railway guard, obstructed from boarding his train as it moved out of Edgware Road station, dashed out into the street and reached Praed Street, the next station, just in time to regain his train!

The second story concerns the Inner Circle, and an elderly lady of ample proportions who found it necessary to alight from a narrow third class compartment in reverse, with her back to the platform. The guard saw her in this position, half in and half out of the compartment, and concluded that she was trying to board the train — so he gave her a helping push. It is said that she travelled the whole Inner Circle, being pushed back into the train at each station, before the guard realised his mistake. One detects a music hall flavour about this story, but withal it would seem that there was more time and opportunity for humour on those railways than there is on our timed-to-a-second tube trains.

And here is a vivid account of a journey on the Inner Circle, made about 1893 by a writer in search of experience who obtained permission to ride on the locomotive footplate of a District Railway train. His journey began with the train rushing into St James's Park station and barely leaving him time to mount the footplate before it plunged into a tunnel on its way to Mansion House.

He experienced a fierce wind, and his ears were assailed by a terrific noise. Innumerable blacks filled his eyes, and in the impenetrable darkness the driver and fireman, and the inspector who accompanied him, all vanished from view. Westminster Bridge, Charing Cross and Temple were all passed before he could think of anything but holding grimly to a rail. The only illumination came from signal lamps and an occasional fierce glow from the firebox as the fireman opened the door to shovel on more coal. After Mark Lane the disused and deserted Tower station was passed on the way to Aldgate, where the fireman jumped down, speedily made arrangements for refilling the water tanks on the locomotive and they were off again before passengers could notice anything more than a brief stop. Two minutes later they rounded a sharp curve to Bishopsgate and then on to Aldersgate (opened in 1865 but not much used until the nearby market opened).

Beyond Aldersgate, sunlight and air entered the tunnel through a series of arches, and then from Farringdon Street to King's Cross, the longest stretch between stations, the train picked up speed until it touched 40mph. The average speed was 20-25mph. As the line turned westward and the gradient steepened, the writer noticed that the air grew steadily more foul (because of defective ventilation) and it was worst in the region of Gower Street station (Euston Square). Even the driver remarked on it, adding that in summertime it was 'killing'. Beyond the junction with the St Johns Wood line at Baker Street (not in use then), the ventilation holes in the tunnel roof gave 'beautiful effects of light striking into darkness', and just before Praed Street the line entered a sort of open air chasm between houses.

Passing trains, of which there were many, were not noticed much except for their lights and the glare from their fires, for the writer's own engine was making too much noise. At High Street Kensington engines were changed, because (so the writer was told and we can well believe) they needed rest periods from the strain of intense working. Also it was the practice to run them in opposite directions as their wheels tended to wear unevenly if the locomotives travelled round and round the Inner Circle for long periods in the same direction.

St James's Park station was finally reached and the 13-mile circuit of the Inner Circle was completed in 70 minutes.* Taking into consideration the frequent stops at stations, 27 of them in all, and the engine change, this was considered good running, as indeed it was in the circumstances. But once round that gloomy tunnelled circuit on the footplate was sufficient for the writer.

Whilst there is very little left to remind us of the original Metropolitan steam railway, a curious relic does exist and can be seen in Bayswater, although no one without foreknowledge would connect it in any way with a railway. It is a dummy house, or rather a dummy pair, Nos 23 and 24 Leinster Gardens, identical with all the other houses and yet having no substance, as it were. Although its frontage is identical, it is merely a wall 5ft thick, complete with fictitious windows and front door (minus letter box) and nothing else. Its purpose is to fill what would otherwise have been an ugly gap in the uniform, dignified frontage of this row of buildings, for at this point the Metropolitan Railway passes beneath.

The Metropolitan was obliged to construct this camouflage to placate owners whose property might have lost value had the gap been left. It has withstood the bombing of London and will continue, maybe for many years,

---

*It takes about 50min to travel the Circle Line today.

to be a source of amusement to those in the know. There are many tales of young innocents being directed to enquire, or deliver something at this queer house, at whose door they stood puzzled until it dawned on them that the door would never open.

Although it is now a matter of past history, the electrification of the Metropolitan and the District systems in 1905 was easily the most important event in their respective lives. It was almost a case of electrification or die, for as steam lines their position was deteriorating rapidly in the face of competition from the recently-opened electric tube railways. Electrification was necessarily a joint undertaking since Inner Circle Metropolitan trains ran over part of the District territory, and in any case their interests had too much in common to allow one railway to electrify without the other.

Eventually the two lines decided to electrify the up and down sections of line between Earls Court and High Street Kensington, as an experiment. This was in 1899, and in the following year a six-coach train comprising two motor coaches and four trailers was tested against a steam-hauled train. The electric train came out of the test with flying colours, and was run on this section of line as a passenger train, the fare being one shilling as against 2d to 4d on the steam train. It was thought that people would pay extra for the experience of riding in an electric train, but in fact the novelty had already worn off since the City & South London Railway had been running electric trains for 10 years, and the train was soon taken off.

Although by this time both companies had decided to go ahead with electrification, it was not to be a straightforward matter of getting the job done quickly, for a dispute arose between the two companies as to the particular electrical system to be adopted. The Metropolitan favoured the Ganz system of high-tension alternating current, which was to be generated at 11-12,000V and stepped down by static transformers to 3,000V, at which pressure it was to be transferred to overhead copper wire conductors.

The Metropolitan's advisers maintained that this system would prove most economical, since it would require no substations and no heavy conductor rail such as would be necessary with a system using low-tension direct current. Another advantage they claimed was that the static transformers required no attendants and could be locked in a room and left to work themselves.

The District, on the other hand, favoured the British Thomson-Houston Company's low-tension system by which direct current was to be fed to conductor rails on the track. The matter was complicated by the fact that the Metropolitan was then financially sound and therefore powerful enough to insist, if necessary, on its own favoured electrical system; whilst the District Railway was practically bankrupt but sincerely believed in the superiority of *its* system.

At this interesting stage there appeared on the scene Charles Tyson Yerkes, an American who for 10 years had financed the equipping of elevated railroads and electric tramways in America. The controlling group of

22

shareholders of the District Railway stock had turned to him for financial help, and their negotiations resulted in the formation of the Metropolitan District Electric Traction Co Ltd, a move which improved the District's financial position and gave it equal bargaining powers with the Metropolitan Railway.

Yerkes refused to act on the expert advice which favoured the Metropolitan system, and even went so far as to visit Budapest to see the Ganz system, which had been applied to a short section of railway there. He did not see it because by this time the experimental section of line had been dismantled, but he did see the 67-mile Valtellina line, which ran from Lecco alongside Lake Como to Sondrio, and whether he was influenced or not as a result, he finally decided that overhead conductors would not suit the London systems. The matter was now a really serious issue between the two companies, and they finally went to arbitration — the Press making great play of the controversy meanwhile. After a long sitting the tribunal appointed by the Board of Trade gave judgement for the dc system, and the tremendous jobs of building great power stations at Lots Road and Neasden and many substations, and laying miles of cable, were at last put in hand.

Some 26 miles in all of the Metropolitan were electrified in three years, a very creditable performance considering the line was clear for workmen for only about six hours out of every 24. The length of the District to be electrified was even more. At first an experimental electrified line between Ealing and South Harrow was laid down and used both for testing the installation and for training crews to operate the new electric trains. Whilst this was going on, the work of electrification was proceeding steadily, and eventually, on 22 September 1905, the last steam train puffed around the Inner Circle. Not many months after its exit the whole programme of electrification of both railways was completed. Henceforth there were long, well-lit saloon coaches for the passengers' delight, and the discomforts of dim and stuffy compartment coaches were done with.

It was as if the authorities wished to wipe the memories of steam trains from the minds of their passengers, for stations and tunnels were thoroughly cleaned of accumulated layers of soot and grime, and there was much repainting and general brightening up of both lines as soon as possible afterwards. The two companies were eager to make their railways more attractive than those of the competitive tube lines.

2
The First Tube Railways

In writing about the growth of London's underground railways, it is difficult to avoid an occasional backward glance through the years. If the story unfolded neatly there would be no excuse for this; but it does not, for more than one brain was grappling with London's traffic problem, and more than one plan took shape and developed at the same time.

'Tube' railways as we know them are driven in so radically different a manner from 'cut and cover' that they might excusably be thought modern, but the basic process of driving a large tunnel without disturbing the surface directly above is old. In the absence of records it is impossible to say just how old it really is; but the first practical instance of it so far as this book is concerned is dated 1843. In March of that year the first tunnel beneath the Thames was opened, connecting Rotherhithe on the south bank with Wapping on the north. Its length was 1,200ft. In fact, it was the first great underwater tunnel in the world.

The engineer responsible was Sir Marc Isambard Brunel, father of the famous Isambard Kingdom Brunel who engineered the Great Western Railway.

Sir Marc's method of tunnel construction employed a rectangular iron shield, shaped like a huge box with open ends, and furnished with projecting teeth. It was placed at the working face of the tunnel, and as the face was gradually excavated the shield was moved forward, protecting men working within against the great pressure of earth above them. The shield was honeycombed with compartments wherein worked miners and bricklayers, and as it moved forward beneath the river bed, the miner excavated the spoil and strengthened the cavity he made, being followed by a bricklayer who lined it with brickwork.

Brunel's tunnel was intended to expedite the work of the London docks and save horse-drawn traffic making the long detour by London Bridge. Long sloping approaches were necessary for this purpose, but when the tunnel was completed the promoting company had no funds left for anything else; and as the tunnel could be approached only by stairways down circular shafts at each end, pedestrians were the only people who could use it. It was an extremely costly project, for there were many setbacks during the working, and the whole job took 18 years to complete, including a seven-year period when it was abandoned through lack of funds. Before this, the Thames had burst through the roof into the workings and drowned seven men, so it is not to be wondered at that Brunel's health broke down before the finish.

Pageantry was introduced into the old tunnel when Brunel himself was preceded by a procession headed by a band of the Coldstream Guards, and subsequently when banquets were held under the river, but the tunnel acquired and retained the name of 'Brunel's White Elephant' until the old East London Railway took it over and projected a steam railway through it in 1869. Incidentally, access to the present London Transport Wapping station is by one of the original large circular shafts of the old tunnel. The lifts are built within it, on a framework, and its size can best be appreciated when seen from the stairways, which run down its inner walls to the platforms. The station has been reconstructed, and, to commemorate Brunel's Thames Tunnel, a slate plaque (recently replaced by a plaque in granite) affixed to a pillar in the reconstructed station bears the words:

The tunnel which runs under the Thames from this station was the first tunnel for public traffic ever to be driven beneath a river. It was designed by Sir Marc Isambard Brunel (1769-1849) and completed in 1843. His son Isambard Kingdom Brunel (1806-1859) was engineer-in-charge from 1825 to 1828

ERECTED BY LONDON TRANSPORT IN 1959

An interesting discovery made during the reconstruction was that of a huge iron chain with 6in links made from 1¼ diameter bar. This encircled the brickwork of the shaft, which was built on a cast iron ring *above* ground to a height of 42ft. As the ground within the ring was cut away, the whole mass of iron and brickwork sank slowly into the earth. Hence the very likely theory that this 120-year-old chain, and maybe others like it, was a necessary girdle to prevent the ring of brickwork collapsing under the strain.

In 1869, also, the engineer Peter Barlow was given the task of driving a second Thames tunnel, this time between the Tower and Bermondsey. He improved on Brunel's method, using a circular shield and dispensing with brickwork, lining the tunnel instead with cast iron segments bolted flange to flange. The Tower Subway, as it was named, had a minimum depth of 22ft as against the shallower Rotherhithe tunnel, but was only 7ft in diameter when completed. Barlow's shield was driven forward through the earth by levers and jacks, cutting into clay and averaging 5ft progress per day.

Both the method of tunnelling and the tunnel itself are notable in railway history, for this iron-lined tube was the first of its kind in the world; and since it later contained a small railway, it was also the very first tube railway. Passengers descended a shaft in a lift, and at the bottom took their seats in a car which was drawn through the tube by cable, worked by a small stationary engine. The rail track gauge was 2ft 6in and the car held 12 passengers.

Brunel's and Peter Barlow's methods were pointers to the scientific tunnelling of today, and from these origins has evolved the famous Greathead shield, which cut most of London's tube tunnels and is used in other parts of the world. James Henry Greathead drove the tunnels for the Stockwell to King William Street tube railway in 1886, and to do so he used a shield of his own design. It differed from Barlow's in so far as it was driven forward into the earth by hydraulic rams or jacks working at a pressure generally of one ton per square inch, although the large Greathead shield used for the Blackwall Tunnel worked at a pressure of 2¾-ton/sq in. The rams pressed against the iron tunnel segments already fixed in place, and forced the 12ft diameter shield into the earth, enclosing a great core which was removed by the miners. The excavated section of tunnel was sprayed with liquid cement, and after a ring of iron plates was placed in position, more cement was forced through the holes in the plates to fill the interstices; the process is known as grouting.

Comparatively recently, however, for an experimental section of tube, an entirely new method of excavation and tunnel lining was used. In the Finsbury Park to Tottenham section of new tunnel incorporated in the Victoria Line, where soft clay soil lent itself to the method, rotating 'drum diggers, were employed. One was of 14ft external diameter for concrete-lined tunnels, and the other, for iron-clad tunnels, 13ft 1in. Essentially the drum digger consists of two drums, one within another. The outer 14ft drum has a bevelled cutting edge and is driven into the tunnel face in a manner similar to that already described. The inner drum of 7ft 6in diameter is rotated on roller races by hydraulic motors. It has cutting teeth mounted on arms on its outer edge, and cuts the area in front of the space between inner and outer drums. The area in front of the inner drum is cut by teeth mounted on an arm across the drum's diameter.

The ram operator is provided with sighting guides to enable him to adjust the pressure on the rams to correct any tendency to deviate right or left or up or down from the prescibed direction or gradient. The clay excavated is guided by scoops or paddles to a belt conveyor and subsequently the clay is discharged into skips on rails for eventual hoisting up the working shafts.

When the outer shield has reached the end of its thrust, a new ring of tunnel lining is added, the rams push against the newly installed ring and the whole cycle recommences. The process for the iron lined tunnels using a 13ft 1in shield, is similar; and with both iron and concrete lined tunnel a far greater speed of excavation over the previous methods was obtained. Much time was saved by the use of cast iron segments with flexible joints, the new method allowing for each completed ring of segments to be expanded by jacks against the clay outside, and finally wedged firmly in place when the pressure on the jacks is released. This method obviated the need for cement grouting with both the iron and cement tunnel linings, as the latter is similarly expanded against the clay.

The foregoing method of tunnelling using drum diggers obviously cannot be used where rocky or otherwise obstructive soil formations are met with, and here, unless some entirely new method is evolved in the future, the only means of winning a passage will be by the non-rotating shield, by mechanical shovel or even by manual excavation.

You may already have heard of instances during the building of new tube lines where two tunnels have been driven towards each other, and have met dead accurately, or within a fraction of an inch. The layman can almost imagine the engineers meeting like Stanley and Livingstone, only deep below-ground, and congratulating one another on their skill. The author's guess is that if the tunnels did *not* meet fairly true the engineers would soon be out of work. Nevertheless, driving tunnels horizontally at deep level entails such precise measurement beforehand that an error of 1/16in in sighting would throw the actual driving seriously out of alignment.

In surveying the intended route of a tube railway, those responsible had in the past to ensure, as far as possible, that no private property was encroached upon, otherwise the property owner would have had to be settled with. This was one of the reasons why tubes followed the course of highways, thereby adding to the length of the tunnel, and often entailing sharp curves such as exist at South Kensington on the Piccadilly Line, where there is a double reverse curve, and at Bank on the Central Line.

Of late years, however, it has been proved that the effect of tunnelling under property is negligible, but the cost of the actual tunnelling having greatly increased, it is cheaper now to drive a tunnel as straight as possible between two points. This also conforms with London Transport's policy to avoid curves sharper than 400-metre radius, thus minimising speed restrictions and obviating tunnels of larger diameter necessary at sharp curves. The proposed tunnel, or twin tunnels in the case of new routes or extensions, may still curve, rise or fall, and there are no means of sighting the progress of work from the surface. Therefore the survey must note surface levels as well as direction, and of course, the position of sewers and service mains likely to be affected along the route.

In due course a series of vertical shafts is sunk, from which headings are driven at right-angles to the line of route. To find the exact centre line along which to bore the running tunnel, a theodolite (an instrument for measuring angles by optical means) is set on the surface over the end of a heading and precisely over the subterranean line of route — but of course far above it. Two plumb lines are next hung down the working shaft, and exactly aligned with a sight on the instrument. The theodolite, thus set, is taken to the bottom of the shaft, and its position adjusted until this time it agrees with the plumb lines already adjusted from above. In other words, a sight line taken above ground is about to be transferred below, and it is only necessary to determine a true right-angle off the vertical plummets and to fix a true depth. When the correct distance along the heading has been measured, and the true right-angle determined, there is the point and direction of the running tunnel's centre line, and work can begin.

The shield is erected in position in a chamber formed by several rings of iron lining, and a short excavation is made in the working face of the running tunnel. Then, if the earth is soft enough for the purpose, piles are inserted between it and the edge of the shield, and a forward thrust of the shield drives the piles into the face and breaks up the earth for easy removal. With the Greathead type of shield it is necessary thereafter to cut a small chamber in the face in advance of the shield, so that the earth enclosed by the ring of the shield after each forward thrust may collapse into the space made.

The greater part of London's tube tunnelling is in general a standard 12ft internal diameter; but for the experimental stretch of running tunnel at Finsbury Park for the Victoria Line it was 12ft 8in and 12ft 6in, using cast iron and concrete respectively for lining. The Victoria Line's tunnels thus lined approximated on straightforward stretches to that increased internal diameter. But we are gradually abandoning the old Imperial linear measure, and the running tunnels of the present Jubilee Line are quoted as 3.85m for those parts lined with cast iron segments, and 3.81m for those line with concrete segments, the latter being 0.75m wide as against 0.6m on earlier lines. The station tunnels are all 6.50m internal diameter with the exception of Baker Street where the diameter is 6.464m. Extra-large shields have been constructed to drive these.

Pedestrian tunnels to and from the platforms are excavated with hand tools and pneumatic spades, etc. These tunnels are of short length, and shields to excavate them would be uneconomical, besides taking more time, as a chamber larger than the shield must necessarily be built in which to erect the shield. The heavy cost, and the time required to erect and dismantle a shield are factors against it use for relatively small jobs. With regard to escalator tunnels, which are also excavated by hand, the case here against the use of a shield is that it would be impossible, or at any rate very difficult, to control a shield on such a slope as that on which an escalator is built.

On certain sections of the London 'tubes' the tunnels may be seen to dip on leaving the stations, and to rise on approach to them; by looking through the end windows, where a sight along the interior of several successive cars can be had, the 'bend' of the train on meeting each rise or fall is markedly perceptible. Wherever practicable, running tunnels are so graded for the double purpose of accelerating the departure of a train and retarding its speed on approach. The falling gradient of about 1 in 30 results in a saving, too, on current consumption; and conversely the rising gradient, which is made rather less acute, means economy in braking material. With modern trains possessing reserves of tractive power and powerful brakes these miniature switchbacks are not so important, although they still appeciably augment the overall speed where stations are close together.

On various occasions when driving tunnels, engineers have had to contend with more than clay or workable earth. They have encountered water-logged sand, or have had to tunnel beneath rivers and streams, were normal tunnelling methods would have resulted in quickly flooded workings. Perhaps the most difficult tube-tunnelling problems met with up to the year 1932 arose outside this country.

For instance, while sinking shafts for the Moscow underground railway, a depth of quicksand was encountered. It was impossible to stem this sliding mass until air had been forced through it under pressure, drying and partially solidifying it long enough for the shaft lining to be bolted into position. On other occasions the sand had to be frozen to the depth of one metre around the shaft, both to hold it in position and keep in check the seeping water. At Victoria station on the Victoria Line, something similar was encountered, but on a smaller scale, in 1964.

So far as London is concerned the general procedure is to construct airtight working chambers and compress the air within them, so that there is sufficient pressure to keep out the water, or in certain cases, to help support the periphery of face of the tunnel. If a waterlogged stratum is met when sinking a shaft, a vertical chamber is constructed; and if a tunnel has to driven through a bed of soaked sand, for instance, then a horizontal chamber is made. In both cases a smaller compartment is constructed at the entrance to the pressure chamber to form an air lock, so that men and material do not enter or leave the pressure chamber direct from the outer air.

The principle is similar to that of a river lock, where when a vessel enters the lock, the gates are closed behind it to allow the lock water to be raised or lowered to the level of the next stretch, and then the forward gates are opened to permit entry to the new level. In the case of an air lock, men and material enter from the outer air, the steel door is closed behind them and the air pressure raised gradually until it equals that in the pressure chamber.

Only then will the inner door be opened; for were it opened earlier there would be an escape of air into the chamber, thus lowering the tunnel pressure and permitting a possible inrush of water. On tube construction work, air pressures vary from 5 to 35lb sq in, but the average is around 10lb sq in.

The greater portion of tunnelling for London's tubes has been driven through what is known as London clay, varying in colour from grey-green to yellow, which lies on top of the chalk and sand that once formed a sea bed. The tunnels burrow beneath shallow beds of gravel and river drift which the Thames and its tributaries have deposited over the clay throughout countless years. Roughly north of a line represented by Euston Road, the London clay comes to the surface, and stretches out as far as the chalk of the Chiltern Hills. In central and southern districts of London, pockets of sand and gravel, sometimes waterlogged, are found lying beneath layers of 'made ground' formed by the foundations of older London. The depth of the made ground is as much as 24ft at Farringdon Street. Under a few parts of London the predominant clay is shallow in depth, and chalk is encountered, but, generally speaking, London rests on a very thick layer of clay that is anything up to 450ft in depth. Had there been rock such as New York is partly built upon, or peaty swamps such as lie beneath Leningrad instead of the stodgy but amenable clay, it is certain that London's tube railways would not have been so extensive as they are today.

The old City & South London Railway, originally known as the City of London & Southwark Subway, was the first practicable tube railway in the world. That is a distinction not without disadvantage, for to bring it in line with London's modern tube system has meant practically rebuilding it. However, its promoters could not have been expected to foresee that contingency when they conceived the idea of a tube railway a century ago. In the first place, their plan was merely for a tube in which the trains were to be cable-operated, to run from King William Street, near the Monument in the City, to the Elephant & Castle in Lambeth, about 1½ miles. The route was, however, considered too short to develop the potential capacity of the line, and after work on it had started in 1886, authority was obtained to extend the line to Stockwell, making it three miles in length. An engine at the Elephant was to have driven two cables, one at 10mph on the sharply curving City section from King William Street, and another, driven at 12mph, on the straighter and easier Stockwell section.

Contracts were arranged for a supply of cable equipment, but the work was never carried out, because in the meantime it had been decided to adopt electricity as the motive power. This was promised to provide a higher average speed, and ultimately to be a cheaper medium, than the cable.

Thus in 1890 the City & South London Railway opened for public traffic. Its trains of three bogie-trailer cars were hauled at an average speed of 11½mph by 12-ton electric locomotives.

Only by their freedom from steam and smoke could these early trains have commended themselves to travellers, for in contrast to the semi-Victorian opulence of the Metropolitan and District steam trains, the City & South London Railway offered little passenger comfort. The function of this 'sardine box railway', as it was dubbed, was merely to take passengers from one station to another without delays from road traffic. This it did with increasing success, as within three years of its opening the line was carrying 15,000 passengers per day. The coaches, appropriately nicknamed 'padded cells', were small and narrow, designed for a tunnel purposely made as small as possible to reduce construction costs. Passengers sat on longitudinal benches, above which were tiny windows that were little more than ventilators, so that in the absence of advertisements, the passengers could do little more than sit and stare at one another. Electric lighting was provided (a comparative luxury compared with the gas lighting of the Metropolitan and District stock), so the fortunates who sat beneath the low-powered bulbs were perhaps able to read their newspapers.

It would be unfair to the memory of this line, however, to let it go at that. It has been properly pointed out that trams, then the only alternative to the tube along that route, had only oil lamps and were less 'well upholstered'.

One of the early locomotives of the C&SLR may still be seen at the South Kensington Science Museum. But for readers to whom the museum exhibit is inaccessible, the only thumbnail picture the author can give is that the locomotives resembled two upright pianos, in iron, placed back to back on wheels. However, it merits more description than this, as it is an intrinsic part of railway history. There were basically two types, represented by Nos 1-14, with flat sides, and No 20 onwards, with rounded sides, which gave more room for the air brake reservoirs.* This was a matter of some moment, since the engines at first carried no air compressor and had to depend for braking on a supply of compressed air taken in at each terminal.

Nos 1 to 14 were built by Mather & Platt, Nos 15-16 by Siemens, and most of the others by Crompton, and all except No 22 were driven by two 50hp motors; No 22 was subsequently (1912) remotored with two 120hp interpole units and was the fastest and most powerful locomotive on the line. All these locomotives had only four wheels on a very short wheelbase, and their overall dimensions were just 14ft by 6ft 6in, by 8ft 6in high. The driving cab extended from front to rear of the locomotive, with the driver facing sideways. Passengers waiting on platforms were thus presented with the odd sight of a driver facing them as the train rumbled in. Compared with the 43-ton Central London Railway locomotives of later days, those of the C&SLR were midgets, but they stood up to many years of hard work, hauling 40-ton trains at speeds of up to 25mph.

These locomotives were designed for a perfectly straight run under known conditions, and were therefore both simple in design and sturdy in build, with a minimum of fittings which could give trouble. Except in No 22, noted above, there was no reduction gear in the drive, and the motor armature was directly mounted on the axle; in short, the vehicle was the absolute embodiment of electric motors on wheels, and these factors no doubt accounted for their long life.

The wiring circuit was straightforward, the driving current merely passing from the collector shoes to a fuse cut-out and main switch, thence to a starting resistance rheostat (or variable control) and through the motors back to earth via the axlebox, wheel and rail. The brakes fitted were of Westinghouse type, operated by compressed air supplied from a tank on the locomotive, the supply being replenished as already stated; later, however, an electrically-driven air compressor was mounted on the locomotive. The train pipe of the brake system was taken over the roofs of the locomotive and its cars. Screw-down-type brakes were also provided.

The device known as the 'dead man's handle', of which more will be said

---

*The precise type(s) represented by locos Nos 11-19 cannot be established. They were the products, respectively, of Siemens, the C&SL itself, Cromptons and Thames Iron Works.

later, had not then been introduced, so a second man, or rather, 'loco boy', as he was called, was carried on the engine, to take control in the event of the driver becoming ill, or otherwise losing control of the train. The second man's normal work included coupling and uncoupling at each journey's end, because here the loco had to run round its train. There were 44 of these electric locomotives in service when the line closed for reconstruction.

Speaking of those days when South Londoners first journeyed to the City on their new electric 'tube', a contemporary writer relates how he descended in a hydraulic passenger lift, to the deep level of the tube, and saw his train come out of the tunnel 'with a roar, emitting sparks from the region of the wheels'. He entered a coach that seated 31 other passengers besides himself and they were all shut in, unable to see what was going on outside because the tiny windows were placed so high as to make this practically impossible. The passengers were informed of the names of approaching stations by the conductor, who raised his voice to a shout so that he could be heard above the noise of the train. It seems that ridicule, more than anything else, wrought a welcome change, and coaches of the next batch were built with larger windows.

The whole of the running line was below ground, as much as 105ft down at the Thames crossing, and never less than 45ft. The workshops and depot were above ground, reached by an inclined ramp at Stockwell, facing towards Brixton. Later, and after an unfortunate mishap when the tow rope broke and the car took a headlong flight back to the main line, the exit slope was abandoned in favour of a lift similar to the one still in use on the Waterloo & City Railway. The up and down running lines had their own separate tunnels, which were only 10ft 2in in diameter from the City to Elephant & Castle (a relic of the intended cable traction), and from there to Stockwell they were four inches larger. At terminal stations they merged into one larger elliptical tunnel.

All the current for the railway was generated in a power house at Stockwell depot, where three dynamos were belt-driven by steam engines which had massive flywheels 14ft in diameter. The current was taken along the tunnels by feeder cable to signal cabins at each station, where other cables led to the conductor rails. The stations and passages were entirely lined with white tiles, except where the space was monopolised by advertisements, and the effect was, to quote from an old record, 'to provide a bright and cheerful gleam under the artificial light'.

The City and South London Railway proved such a popular means of conveyance that its owners grew really worried about the increasing number of passengers, To keep them within workable limits, it was decided to raise the fare (which was 2d for any distance, and no tickets — passengers paid at a turnstile) between the hours of 08.00 and 10.00; but this early example of a peak hour surcharge proved unnecessary after the company improved its signalling system and was able to run a more frequent service of trains.

The line continued to attract more passengers, and before long the small single-road terminus at King William Street became overcrowded. Another site at Lombard Street was therefore chosen, and here the now famous Bank Station was built in 1900, and connected by a new line diverging from the old one near London Bridge. In the next two years the tube was extended south to Clapham Common and north to Moorgate, after which it continued beneath the line of City Road to the Angel at Islington, and subsequently reached King's Cross and Euston by following the slope of Pentonville Road. When the Bank station opened, King William Street Station was left isolated on a short spur and was closed to passengers. So was City Road station many years later, but both remain below ground, dark and deserted except for a period during the last war, when they were once again lit up and used as air raid shelters.

Traffic continued to increase in the years preceding World War 1, until it became obvious that the C&SL Railway would have to be completely modernised. This meant the installation of a new signalling system, the enlargement of stations to take longer trains — which themselves would have to be enlarged — and, of course, the reconstruction of the twin tunnels to an increased diameter; the last a formidable task entailing such a tremendous cost as to put it far beyond the means of the company to carry out unaided. Therefore an agreement was sought and obtained with the Underground Electric Railways Company, which already controlled many of the new tube lines built by then, and the C&SL Railway passed to the control of the UERC, whose finances were better calculated to meet the cost of the inevitable reconstruction.

The first world war, in that tiresome way of all major wars, prevented the job from being carried out forthwith, and regular travellers had to make the best of their undersized railway until 1922, when the work of enlarging the tunnels to the then standard diameter of 11ft 8¼in began. In 1923 the whole line had to be temporarily closed due to a subsidence and buses ran a connecting service, but on completion the way was open for the absorption of the old City & South London Railway into a larger tube system. By the agreement just mentioned it had lost its identity, but from this first tube railway grew the extensive Northern Line, which, in turn, under the present grouping nomenclature, absorbed another early tube line, the Great Northern & City Railway.

This was opened in 1904, running from Finsbury Park, on the Great Northern Railway main line, to Moorgate, with intermediate stations at Drayton Park, Highbury, Essex Road, and Old Street; a total length of only 3½ miles.

The GN & City tube is most interesting to the railway historian, for it was planned as an extension of the Great Northern Railway, whereby rolling stock of main line dimensions from the suburbs and even beyond would have left the surface at Finsbury Park and continued at deep level to the Moorgate terminus. The tunnels were built 16ft in diameter, the largest on any tube system in London. This ambitious plan did not materialise, but an even more ambitious project did eventually! The original plan was modified and altered to fit in with the 1945-50 plan for the expansion of London's transport, but it proved subsequently to be unrealistic in the light of modern conditions, and was eclipsed in fact by events that ended control of the line by London Transport.

An extra powerful Greathead shield was used to drive the tunnels on this line, and partly, it is understood, to reduce cost, the lower cast-iron segments were removed as the tunnel progressed and replaced with a blue brick invert. The stations were built to accommodate long trains of GN stock, and with a length of 420ft at intermediate stations and 450ft at the termini, they always appeared immense and deserted — as indeed they were to some extent, for such long trains never used them. The author has personal memories of travelling daily on this line. In the evening rush hours the cars, built to main line loading gauge, would be crowded, and passengers would overflow on to the end entrance platforms, with little to look at but a large gloomy tunnel, seen through the iron lattice gates. Another memory of this line is of the hydraulic lifts at Finsbury Park and Highbury, descending slowly with a peculiar hissing sound as of water leaking through a burst main.

The cars, like those on the Central London, had open-end platforms where the guard used to stand and work the trellis car gates by levers. There were also sliding doors in the middle of each car, but these were opened only from the outside, and then only at the termini, by porters specially detailed for the job. A seven-car train consisted of three motor-cars and four trailers. Current was supplied from the line's own power station, whose midway position on the route, in a turning off New North Road, allowed for direct cables to be run to four connections along the line, thus making substations unnecessary. When the Metropolitan in 1913 took over from the company owning the line (in which the GN naturally had an interest), it provided its own electricity supply, and demolished the old power station.

For years there was no running connection between the former Great Northern & City Line and any other. One could travel on it between Finsbury Park and Moorgate and that was all. Then in 1960 work began on the Victoria Line construction which eventually severed the low-level connection at Finsbury Park. Consequently the line became a simple shuttle between Moorgate and Drayton Park until it was handed over to British Rail in 1975, to become an integral part of the Great Northen Suburban Electrification Scheme. The execution of this scheme or project takes the old GN & City right out of this book, so at this point it may be interesting to record the unusual route taken by the old rolling stock of this line when it was due for periodic overhaul at Neasden, and when it was finally removed to make way for the newer and smaller stock of standard 'tube' dimensions.

The stock was too large to negotiate the tunnels between Baker Street and

Finchley Road, through which it would normally have had to pass to reach Neasden. So it had to take a roundabout route. It was hauled up to the main L&NE line via a connecting spur at Finsbury Park, and from there reached Aldersgate via King's Cross. It was then hauled in the reverse direction over the Metropolitan Railway via King's Cross to Paddington, thence to Acton Town and out to Rayners Lane Junction, and eventually back over the Metropolitan Railway to Neasden. For its final removal, when it was routed to Chesterfield for scrapping, the old stock took the same route to Neasden, where it was to be stripped of its electrical gear before being taken on the final stage north.

Although the Waterloo & City Railway is not nearly so important a line as the others already mentioned, and is, in fact, an isolated entity and part of the Southern Region of British Rail, it has the distinction of being the second oldest of London's tubes. It is also one that many Londoners have never travelled, although they have lived all their lives in London. The main purpose of this railway, ever since it was planned in 1893, has been to cater for the demands of a specialised section of the public who travelled daily to Waterloo, and then onwards to their City offices.

Well over 100 years ago the London & South Western Railway Company, with its terminus at Waterloo, intended to extend its line to London Bridge, to provide a main-line route almost to the heart of the City, but such an extension was never carried out. The advent of the City & South London Railway proved that tubes were possible and practical, and suggested the idea of a similar but shorter tube from Waterloo to the City, a much less costly project than an extension of the main line. It was duly opened in 1898, and worked by the LSWR, which persuaded Dugald Drummond, its redoubtable locomotive superintendent, to design an electrical shunter that is now in the National Railway Museum's collection at York.

The southern terminus is beneath Waterloo station, although the line extends a little beyond to its sidings and sheds in an open cutting. Here is situated the small power station which supplied electricity to the line before the Southern Region supply system was connected, and a short distance from Waterloo on the City side is the 30ton hoist by which the stock is raised when necessary to the Waterloo main line sidings. There are no intermediate stations, and the journey time from end to end is only five minutes. The line runs first under York Road and them beneath Stamford Street, to pass obliquely under the Thames near Blackfriars Bridge. Thence it follows the line of Queen Victoria Street to the Bank, a total length of 1 mile 46 chains, making it the shortest tube railway in London. At the Bank, its station is connected to the main booking hall of the Central and Northern 'tubes' by a long inclined tunnel, whilst at Waterloo it is reached by escalators serving also the Northern and Bakerloo Lines.

The problem of noisy running on this line was tackled in a new way. To deaden it as much as possible the iron tunnel segments were filled with concrete, making a flush wall; in recent years a further anti-noise measure has been taken by welding running rails into 315ft lengths. Noise, be it added, is a bugbear associated with all tube travel, and varied attempts have been made to combat it on other lines.

This was the first tube line in this country to use motored car rolling stock, a definite breakaway from the locomotive haulage of the City & South London. As it turned out, these motor-cars, built in America and assembled (with British electrical equipment) at the LSWR Eastleigh works, were soundly enough constructed to keep up a regular daily service for over 40 years, until they were all withdrawn in 1940 to make way for new green and aluminium-painted stock, complete with air-operated doors. To facilitate single-car working (which still operates on this line during slack hours), the motor-cars of this stock are fitted with a driving cab at each end.

The Waterloo & City line has several distinguishing features that make it interesting to railway enthusiasts. The trains, for instance, are made up of only five cars, comprising two motor-cars and three trailers; the floors of the motor-cars are on two levels, as they were in the original stock, the raised portion providing space beneath for the switchgear and larger-than-normal motor-bogie wheels. Current is supplied to the motors by a third outer rail and returns via the running rails, thus differing from the London Transport four-rail system, but conforming with the ex-Southern Railway's system of transmission. Waterloo & City trains are thus able to run under their own power on the Southern lines, as indeed they do both for trials, and when they are en route to depots, for painting or attention to coachwork. Repairs to the running gear and driving equipment are carried out at the railway's Waterloo depot.

New signalling equipment was installed when the new rolling stock was introduced, and the line is now track-circuited throughout, with two-aspect colour-light signals and repeaters, electro-pneumatic train stops, and points mechanisms. The latter are at the Bank terminus, where they and the signals are worked automatically as trains arrive and depart. The system directs trains to each platform alternatively so as to even out the wear on the points in the scissor crossing, afterwards reversing the points and clearing the starting signal (if the road is clear) for them to depart. At Waterloo, however, a signalman works the ground pattern lever frames. Further to illustrate the distinctive features of this railway, the tube tunnels are 1¾in larger in diameter that the London Transport predominantly 12ft tube system. The original livery of Waterloo & City stock was dark 'invisible' green.

In 1960 the first moving walkway in this country, called the 'Trav-o-lator', was opened, which eliminated the long, wearisome walk along the foot tunnel previously referred to. It carries many more passengers than did the old foot tunnel, and there is no doubt that some astonishing records have been set up between top and bottom by the old and not-so-old commuters using it.

By the side of the inclined foot tunnel an iron segment-lined tunnel was driven on the same plane, with a gradient of 1 in 7, and of about the same length, 300ft. The tunnel diameter is 16½ft, widening to 19½ft at the lower end to house the 'Trav-o-lator's' return mechanism, and to 29½ft lower still to encompass existing passenger and siding tunnels and generally make things easier for rush hour traffic.

In order partly to make way for a new sub-surface ticket hall and a connecting subway to Poultry, a 4ft sewer, gas and water mains, and various cables had to be diverted. Add to this the removal of very old in-fill material roughly where the Walbrook once flowed underground, and the fact that the new ticket hall's roof is almost at surface level, illustrates the exacting nature of job at this congested junction of City steets. The writer was made aware of it when he was shown the works below ground, especially when it was explained that the violent pounding above his head at one point was the passage of buses and other vehicles overhead.

The next tube line to be built after the Waterloo & City was the Central London Railway, which was opened for public service in 1900. Like the City & South London, it has been re-named (the Central Line) and many miles have been added at each end of its original limits. The Central was at first built entirely in tunnel, and since it runs right across Central London from east to west, there was never much fear that it would fail from lack of passengers. The terms 'popular' and 'populous' can both be ascribed to it. At first one could go anywhere on this line for 2d, and although fares were brought in line with other railways after the colossal drop in traffic of over 2,000,000 passengers during the six months ending June 1907, as a result of competition from the new motorbuses, the name 'Twopenny Tube' clung for many years.

Its route was from the Bank, westward practically in a straight line to Shepherd's Bush, a distance of 5¾ miles. With such stations as Bond Street, Oxford Circus and Holborn on its route, serving London's most famous shopping centres, it was assured of a steady stream of passengers all day. In the morning and evening it catered largely for business folk, and during the day the ladies found it very convenient for reaching the West End shops. The position has altered little with the years, and today, with the line touching north-south London tube routes at Bond Street, Oxford Circus, Tottenham Court Road, Holborn and the Bank, the stations are busier than ever.

There were several innovations on the old Central Line, resulting from successful and not-so-successful attempts to benefit from the experiences of the previous tubes. Thus the island-type platform was not used, for where the twin tubes are on the same level at station sites, they are separated widely enough to allow a platform each, with an intervening wall pieced by cross passages. Where the streets above were narrow, and the contractors were chary about burrowing beneath buildings, the tubes were driven on different levels so that they ran one above the other. In station areas the lines 'switch-backed' into and out of the stations on the principle previously mentioned.

The stations were white tiled and had large nameboards in white enamel on blue, but in addition to this method of identification the train guards would call out the name of the next station on leaving the previous one, and repeat the name upon arrival there. Now, of course, the station name is repeated in notices all along the platform wall, and on the opposite wall at intervals.

In the matter of light and comfort the Central trains were roomier than, and far superior to, those on the City & South London — although the Central, in providing electric locomotives to haul its trains, followed existing example and thereby created difficulties. The Central London tubes (11ft 8¼in in diameter) and trains were larger than those of the City & South London, and as the trains were made up of seven large cars, they needed heavy and powerful locomotives.

There were several disadvantages in this type of traction, of which only two need be mentioned. First, the locomotives took up a good deal of valuable platform space. It has been said that drivers mitigated this evil by drawing up with the locomotive just beyond the platform and within the tunnel. But a contemporary repudiated this for two reasons: it would have meant passing the old manual semaphore signals at danger; and furthermore drivers were forbidden to look out of the cab in the tube! The second disadvantage was that the locomotives were heavy machines and the vibration they caused damaged not only the track, but also the tempers of property owners along the surface. The locomotives vanished early in 1903, but their employment had had one good result, for it originated a series of most valuable experiments to improve the multiple-unit stock. Motors were installed actually on the train in existing trailers partly converted to suit, in the proportion of two motors to each end car, and these were powerful enough to drive a train of six cars. Later on, when the early rolling stock was replaced by some transferred from other lines, motors were distributed intermediately along the train to increase speed and acceleration.

The vibration difficulties practically disappeared with the introduction of motor-cars, but much valuable passenger space was still taken up by the control equipment and switchgear which were housed above the coach frame.

The Central locomotives were of the double-bogie type, with a centrally placed cab and sloping front and rear ends to house the resistances. Although the original locomotives weighed 43 tons each, a subsequent type was built that weighed only 31 tons, of which two thirds was spring-borne and one-third was borne directly on the axles. This weight sufficed to give adhesion to the rails for hauling heavy trains, even though the total weight of the locomotive had been reduced.

These power units hauled trains of coaches in which could plainly be seen the forerunner of tube stock of later days — long, low carriages with a platform at each end enclosed by a lattice gate structure with slightly bowed sides and clerestory roof (a double-tiered roof with wide vents) partly to give more headroom and partly to increase ventilation. The coaches were painted chocolate with a cream band on which the title 'Central London' appeared. The half-hexagonal roof at the leading end of the motor coach was a Central London characteristic.

The Central London Railway was extended westward from Shepherd's Bush to Wood Lane in 1908, in order to serve the Franco-British Exhibition, and eastward in 1912 from the Bank to Liverpool Street to connect with Liverpool Street station. In 1920 the line was brought to the surface beyond Wood Lane, and from there extended to Ealing Broadway, using the GW tracks for part of the distance. Subsequent extensions reached to West Ruislip in the west and Epping in north-east, a distance of 34 miles and a route mileage of 45 miles, including the Hainault loop. To this must be added the 6-mile single-track line from Epping to Ongar, worked by electric shuttle trains since 1957. The whole has now been named the Central Line.

A remarkable piece of equipment at Wood Lane station was a movable platform extension, installed when it became necessary to accommodate the six-car trains needed to deal with sporting crowds attending the White City Stadium.

The requisite elongation of the platform had to foul a spur to the car depot, therefore the extension took the form of a swing span that could be swung round clear of the depot track. It was operated by electro-pneumatic mechanism controlled from a signalbox, and properly inter-locked with the running signals.

The platform, its mechanism, and the station too, have now been swept away. The work involved was interesting: in fact, from an engineering point of view there have been some extremely interesting developments on the Central Line in recent years, and they are well worth more detailed investigation at a later stage.

When several small concerns combine into one large undertaking, they usually do so to effect economy in working. The London Electric Railways Company was such an undertaking, formed in 1910 to combine the activities of several independent tube railways that were not doing too well on their own. They were known before the amalgamation as the Baker Street & Waterloo; the Charing Cross, Euston & Hampstead; and the Great Northern, Piccadilly & Brompton Railways, but eventually they became better known as the Bakerloo, the Hampstead and the Piccadilly tubes.

To detail the early history of each line would make tedious reading, so perhaps it will be sufficient at this stage to mention only the principal events in their careers. These railways in the early days of independent working showed little promise of ever being successful: in fact, although tunnelling for the Baker Street and Waterloo Railway was begun from a north riverside site at Hungerford Bridge on the Thames as early as 1898, and twin underwater tunnels were completed by 1901, work was suspended for a time through lack of financial support.

It was at this somewhat bleak period in London's tube railway history that there arrived from America Charles Tyson Yerkes, the railway specialist, who has been referred to in connection with the electrification of the Twin Lines. Having dealt with this business, he next turned his attention to the formation of a finance company with the three tube lines under its control; and this move, restoring confidence in the projects, allowed work to be started or resumed. Thus, by 1906, the Bakerloo was opened from Baker Street to Kennington Road (now Lambeth North), the Great Northern, Piccadilly & Brompton line was opened from Hammersmith to Finsbury Park, and a year later the Hampstead line was opened from Charing Cross to Golders Green and Highgate (now Archway). In 1910, the financial controlling interests were merged in the London Electric Railways Company, as has been stated. The GNP&B was responsible for at least one innovation that our expensive days would quail at: each station had its own distinctive colour for its tickets.

Since those early years the Bakerloo reached out via Queens Park and the former LNWR tracks to Watford, and in another direction via Wembley Park to Stanmore. However, its present extent is more modest, from Elephant & Castle in the south to Harrow & Wealdstone in the north. Services north of Harrow are now provided solely by British Rail, while the Stanmore branch is incorporated in the Jubilee line. The Piccadilly has extended considerably and boasts those very long runs from Uxbridge and Heathrow in the west to Cockfosters in the north (32 and 30 miles respectively). The Hampstead and Highgate tube has also developed, and with the old City & South London, now forms the Northern Line, stretching from Edgware and Barnet to Morden, and incidentally providing the world for many years with its longest railway all in tunnel.

Left:
The official party previewing the Metropolitan Railway in a contractor's train. Mr and Mrs Gladstone are in the group nearest the camera. *LRT*

3
The System Reaches Maturity

So far, the theme of this book has been the origin and early days of London's Underground Railways, and from now on they can be referred to by their present-day names, which have preserved some measure of individuality despite the fact that they are parts of one vast system.

In reaching out into the country, these lines have undergone great changes. New stations have been built and old ones rebuilt or modernised; and to deal with newly-tapped sources of traffic, surface routes have been integrated with the Underground system, new tunnels driven, lines duplicated, and flying junctions and new viaducts constructed. The huge programme of work outlined just prior to World War II has largely been completed, although parts of it were not concerned primarily with the Underground system, and referred, for instance, to electrification of suburban surface lines into London, and conversion of tram services to trolleybus services. Parts of it, too, were found to be unrealistic in the light of changed circumstances obtaining after the war, which long delayed their consideration. Thus Denham, Elstree and Alexandra Palace were places proposed to be included in the Underground network, but never were. The long-distance extensions were dropped largely because of green belt policies, which curtailed the traffic growth the lines were designed to exploit.

The work just referred to, known as the 1935-40 new works programme, included much alteration and improvement of the Metropolitan Line; but before describing some of its interesting details it will be as well to mention in brief what has happened to the Metropolitan system since electrification, and thus bring its picture a little more up-to-date.

A branch line was opened from Harrow to Uxbridge (1904), Baker Street Station was rebuilt and enlarged (1912), and a year later the Great Northern & City line was taken over. Then followed two long consecutive periods without events of note; one until 1925, when the line was electrified from Harrow to Rickmansworth and the branch to Watford opened; and another until 1932, when a branch line was opened to Stanmore, leaving the main line beyond Wembley Park and passing through Kingsbury and Queensbury. This line was later switched to the Bakerloo system and ultimately to the Jubilee Line. Trains to Aylesbury were until September 1961 worked by steam locomotives north of Rickmansworth, where electric locomotives which hauled compartment stock thus far from Liverpool Street, where uncoupled ready for the return trip. 1960 saw the electrification of the line as far as Amersham, together with the Chesham branch, and, in 1961, Amersham became the terminus of Metropolitan Line trains, leaving the stations beyond to be served by the London Midland Region of British Railways, which took over responsibility for this section of line and increased the service, with Marylebone as the London terminus. Trains on this service are of diesel multiple-unit type, with some first-class accommodation. Interchange is easy with Metropolitan trains at several stations from Harrow northwards.

Thus has ceased the last of the steam-hauled London Transport passenger trains on any part of the Underground. The oldest London Transport passenger vehicles have not ceased giving service, however. Four of the 60-year old coaches that used to operate on the Chesham line are now taken over by the Bluebell Railway Co for their 4½-mile line in Sussex. The only coach otherwise extant is accommodated in the London Transport Museum at Covent Garden.

In comparison with other London Transport lines, the Metropolitan lends itself to long runs at high speeds, especially since a portion of the line has been re-arranged and widened (an interesting piece of railway construction). To exploit this as much as was possible, trains composed of multiple unit compartment stock were fitted with extra-powerful motors, and with these speeds of 60mph were attained. Trains of this type normally ran between Rickmansworth or Watford and Baker Street and Aldgate. With the electrification extension and reorganisation of the line, however, new stock was introduced and will be referred to later. The fact that electric locomotive haulage was also successfully used on this line for many years until 1961 calls for some explanation, perhaps, seeing that the Central London withdrew its locomotives after a short period. The differences in running conditions between the two lines, however, furnish the answer. Locomotives on the Central London could not accelerate or stop the train rapidly enough to suit the closeness of the stations, and maintain the desired high average speed.

The long run on the Metropolitan line to Rickmansworth (13.13 miles non-stop from Finchley Road) was not so much hampered in this way, although at the London end stations are fairly close together. Electric locomotives used on this run were therefore specially designed to work under extremely divergent conditions, being able to accelerate rapidly where the stations are closely situated, and also to maintain high speeds on the more open stretches. In their heyday they could haul trains of an average weight of 180 tons at speeds up to 65mph.

The first electric locomotives for the Metropolitan Railway were built between 1904 and 1906 by the Metropolitan Carriage & Wagon Co, and were somewhat like the Central London locos, although larger. They were of the Bo-Bo type, on two four-wheel bogies, and were intended for hauling Great Western main line trains between Bishops Road (Paddington) and Aldgate.

A second type, more exclusively for the Metropolitans' own use, followed in 1907, and was also of the Bo-Bo type, but with a box superstructure which gave it the appearance of a luggage van. Both types were replaced by 20 new locomotives built in 1922 by Metropolitan-Vickers. These were ultimately adorned with brass nameplates commemorative of celebrated characters, mostly connected with the area served by the Metropolitan, popularly known as Metroland.

They were equipped with 300hp motors, one geared to each of the four axles, with electromagnetic control. Besides the 12 current collector shoes on the locomotive, other shoes were distributed along the train, and connected by a power cable, thus enabling the train to bridge gaps in the conductor rail at crossings and points. The overall length of the locomotive was 39½ft, and its total weight 61½ tons. It could be driven from either end, and was equipped with dual brakes, vacuum and compressed air (Westinghouse). Trip-cocks for train control (a separate one for each type of brake), similar in action to those on multiple-unit trains, were fitted to all engines.

One of these locomotives was exhibited, together with some Metropolitan rolling stock, at the Wembley Empire Exhibition in 1925. For years it carried commemorative plates, but during the war all the locomotives lost their nameplates and their smart lake livery gave place to grey. In 1953-54 the lake livery was restored, as were the nameplates (but in aluminium) on 15 of the remaining 16 locomotives. One of these is preserved in the London Transport Museum and one other is still in departmental use.

The severing of the Stanmore branch from the Metropolitan system and its connection to the Bakerloo Line resulted in improved working for both lines, but, as can be imagined, a great deal of extremely complicated work was involved. There were several motives for this switch-over, one of which was that the districts served by the Stanmore branch had become fairly densely populated long before the last war, and more and more passengers used the Metropolitan Line to reach the West End of London; but to do so they had to change to the Bakerloo, thus causing congestion at Baker Street station.

The new scheme involved the construction of entirely new double tubes branching off the Bakerloo system in 1939 at Baker Street, and proceeding along and beneath the line of the Metropolitan for 2½ miles to a point at Finchley Road station, where they had to rise to the Metropolitan level. A rearrangement of the latter's tracks allowed Bakerloo trains to continue thence, using the two Metropolitan tracks to Wembley Park, where beyond the station they branch off to Stanmore by means of a 'dive-under' junction.

At Baker Street this work required a new tube junction and escalators, etc, and a new southbound tube platform, so that Bakerloo trains from Watford and Queens Park and those from Stanmore could enter the station together. In the same programme, all the Bakerloo stations had to be lengthened to take seven-car trains instead of six, and at Elephant & Castle terminus a new length of double tube siding had to be constructed to provide adequate facilities for reversing.

As part of the plan the Metropolitan services into and out of Baker Street were to be speeded up by allowing the trains a clear run of several miles without intermediate stops — and with a new tube running beneath the Metropolitan Line and relieving much of its load, this was made possible.

On the much congested stretch of Metropolitan Line between Finchley Road and Baker Street, three Metropolitan stations — Lords, Marlborough Road and Swiss Cottage — were closed and two deep-level tube stations, Swiss Cottage and St Johns Wood, were built on the Bakerloo in replacement. The closure of the three stations mentioned made it possible for all 'Met' trains to run non-stop from Baker Street to Finchley Road.

At Finchley Road a remarkable feat of engineering was performed. The point where the new Bakerloo running tubes were to emerge had to lie *between* the Metropolitan tracks, and this meant constructing a new south-bound Metropolitan tunnel further out. The new northbound Bakerloo tube then rose through the abandoned tunnel after the Metropolitan trains had been diverted to their new tunnel.

In fact, this work might well have been called 'Operation Beer Cellar', for the new Metropolitan tunnel had to be dug close under buildings fronting Finchley Road, and in addition to the task of diverting sewers and gas and water mains, a hotel had to be completely underpinned by men working from its basement. This was the 'North Star' hotel, and its cellars had only two inches of concrete separating them from the crown of the new tunnel when it was completed.

Another tricky problem was met with whilst rebuilding Finchley Road station. A great steel girder, 50ft in length, on which the building rested and under which the trains ran, was found to be partly in the way of the new ticket hall. Rather than remove the entire girder, a strengthening flange was welded on to it to compensate for the section of the top of the girder that had to be cut away.

All this time the station was in constant use and the train service was not interrupted. It is rather awesome to imagine that if any serious miscalculation had been made, the whole building might have collapsed on to the line. But such things never do happen, for they are too expertly planned beforehand.

Beyond Finchley Road to Harrow the Metropolitan tracks had to be rearranged, partly in connection with an altered layout at Harrow, but principally so that the Bakerloo lines could run between them as far as Wembley Park, thus allowing fast Metropolitan trains to travel non-stop between Finchley Road and Wembley Park, leaving the intermediate stations to be served by the Bakerloo stopping trains. The question of how the two Bakerloo tracks were to leave the Metropolitan Line at Wembley Park for Stanmore, without crossing the Metropolitan on the level and thereby causing delays, was solved by a 'dive-under' crossing whereby Bakerloo trains could under-pass the southbound Metropolitan tracks, and at the same time another dive-under, constructed south of Wembley Park station, allowed Bakerloo trains access to the nearby Neasden Depot and also enabled Metropolitan trains to work between the latter and the northbound Metropolitan slow track.

In assessing the magnitude of the Metropolitan Line improvement scheme and the projection of the Bakerloo Line to Stanmore, not only has this work to be considered, but also work on new and rebuilt stations, trackwork and signalboxes. And there was also the formidable task of underpinning surface buildings where new tunnels passed close beneath. At Baker Street, where the new tubes joined the parent Bakerloo Line, a 'step plate' junction had to be built around the existing tunnels, without interrupting their traffic, and probably, none of the passengers knew that they were travelling through an iron pipe supported in the very bowels of the earth. When it came to removing the smaller tunnels, however, the work could not be done with trains running, and had to be restricted to the small hours between 1am and 5am. The complicated planning of the scheme, and the tremendous effort involved, were worthwhile. They resulted in a new and faster service north of Baker Street, and the clearing from that station of as many as 160 trains per hour.

The final part of the 1935-40 programme as it affected the Metropolitan Line was electrification of the line beyond Rickmansworth to Amersham and Chesham. This part of Buckinghamshire was being steadily developed and the present and expected population needed something more than steam-hauled services operating north of Rickmansworth.

Before such electrified services could operate from Amersham and Chesham to their best advantage, it was imperative to eliminate a bottleneck consisting of the one pair of tracks which perforce carried all traffic: fast Metropolitan, local Metropolitan and main line British Railways express, local and goods between Harrow on the Hill and the junction of the Watford branch between Moor Park and Rickmansworth.

Two extra tracks were built between these points, mainly to the east of the existing line, and the whole scheme involved the rebuilding or widening of seventeen bridges as well as alterations to stations. The section is now four-tracked throughout, with the new tracks carrying the fast Metropolitan and British Railways trains, leaving the old tracks for local Metropolitan services. The work allowed for an increased and faster Metropolitan service generally. As part of the 1935-40 programme it had been delayed by the advent of World War II intervening, and was not re-started in fact until 1958.

The history of the line has seen a long era of steam locomotive haulage supplemented as from 1905 by electric locomotive haulage, and now British Railways trains and London Transport electric multiple-unit trains fill the picture. The improved services, made possible by reconstruction and the introduction of new rolling stock, operate on the clock-face principle, giving departures at regular intervals, at so many mninutes past each hour. To people living and intending to live in the Rickmansworth to Amersham and Chesham districts, and even beyond as far as Aylesbury, this has proved to be a boon. London Transport did in fact issue to the public an interesting pamphlet illustrating the project, and to all enlightened people concerned it must have been a welcome gesture. Such notices to the public not only have the ring of authenticity, they also enrol an anonymous army of understanding folk who appreciate being taken into London Transport's confidence, in the latter's efforts to provide the best possible services for the travelling public.

More recently, plans have been announced for the closure of Marylebone station and the revision of train services. Should this take place, the Underground would be responsible for all services south of Amersham.

The District Line also has something interesting to offer in the way of complicated and large-scale projects, for the reconstruction work carried out some years ago at Aldgate and Aldgate East decidedly comes within this category. This work in particular will be described. Reference to the other projects that came later, as part of a £2,750,000 scheme to modernise the eastern section of the District Line, will help to bring the picture of this line up to date. Actually, there was no mention in the 1935-40 New Works Programme of any extension or development of the District, except the work at Aldgate.

It has already been mentioned that in 1932 the District services were extended to Upminster. This is half-way to Southend, but it is interesting to recall that as early as 1910 there were through trains running from Ealing to Southend which were hauled as far as Barking by electric locomotives, where steam haulage took over, the old London, Tilbury & Southend Railway supplying the motive power. Also in that year a District service commenced running to Uxbridge via Rayners Lane, and it was thus possible to travel by electric train, with only one change, from Uxbridge to Barking, a distance of more than 30 miles.

The District electric locomotives of those days were powerful but not very distinguished in appearance. Angular, like the coaches they headed, they were often to be seen coupled in pairs hauling the heavy Southend trains. They were scrapped some time after the through service to Southend was discontinued in 1939.

It was on this east-west line, near Aldgate where the Inner Circle Line converges, that delays to traffic occurred owing to insufficient manoeuvring space, and the track and tunnel layout had to be altered. It was a first-rate example of reconstruction and alteration carried out under extremely difficult conditions, without interruption to a full and frequent service of trains. In particular, the rebuilding of Aldgate East station and its re-siting further to the east, which took the best part of three years from 1936 onwards, can rightly be termed a remarkable piece of engineering.

On the map the present station can be seen lying east of the Metropolitan and District railway triangle at Aldgate. Before reconstruction, delays occurred through trains already in Aldgate East station fouling the spur line and the points controlling it, for two sides of the triangle were only long enough to accommodate six-car trains. It was to lengthen these sides to take eight-car trains (by utilising the space occupied by the old platforms), as well as to provide better passenger facilities and a larger station, that the work of re-siting the station some 500ft to the east was undertaken.

To get the required headroom for two new ticket halls, beneath Whitechapel Road, one at each end of the new station, the tracks had to be considerably lowered. The work of enlarging the tunnel, which included installing girders up to 68ft in length to take the overhead weight of Whitechapel Road and its traffic, had to be done without interfering either with the trains or with the road traffic, and required extreme care because many of the surface buildings were old and more liable to collapse.

The big fishbelly girders spanning the line and part of the platform were brought there by road, and lowered into the space where the tunnel crown had been demolished. The longer and heavier girders for the reconstruction work further west (those spanning the new four-track layout at the site of the old station) had to be brought to the job in halves. They came on special crocodile trucks — arriving each Saturday night when the service stopped — the north half-girder being brought along the old north track and the south half along the south track, travelling lengthways through the tunnels. They were halted beneath the appointed position and swung round on ball races, so that they straddled both platform and track. Then one end of each half-girder was led into a chase cut into the new retaining walls, and the other end was bolted to its fellow to make the complete girder. The whole immense steel beam was then raised into position, and a few hours later trains were running beneath!

But it was the method adopted for lowering the track in the new station that captured the imagination. Whilst the new station was being built, and until it was nearly ready for use, the tracks were left at their original level, except for a slight initial lowering to make room for the new girders. Passengers in the trains could see the new-level platforms by looking right down: but few of them knew that they were running over a temporary viaduct, in the shape of a long wooden trestle, which supported the track whilst the ground was dug away from underneath.

When all was ready, a 1,400ft length of double track was lowered a maximum of 7ft! To do this the tracks were first suspended from the roof, then the trestles were dismantled, and the tracks let down with blocks and tackle. This work began at 1 o'clock on a Sunday morning, soon after the traffic had ceased, and thereafter the station must have presented a scene of tremendous activity, for a great deal more work had to be done in the brief Sunday hours remaining.

The old station platforms were demolished; the ticket hall, left incomplete because it fouled the old tracks, was made entire; signalling was installed and tested; and at 5 o'clock on Monday morning the first train came through on the new level. On this complicated operation 900 men were employed, and the train service was interrupted for only one day.

As part of the modernisation of the District Line's eastern section, track rearrangements carried out by British Railways, Eastern Region, eliminated the flat junctions at Barking, and both District and main line services now have independent tracks. Some 700 District and main line trains use the junctions at Barking daily, and delays in the past were frequent, as one would expect. Modernisation of the District Line has resulted in improved running throughout the line in both East and West London.

On the Central London Railway, now the Central Line, no event of particular interest took place between 1920 when the line reached Ealing, and the late 1940s, when it was extended eastwards and westwards. It was then transformed from a short inner suburban line into a veritable railway system on its own, extending miles into the country on either side of London.

There were two main reasons for the western projection: one, to balance the workings in the west with those in the east, where the line thrusts out into Essex; the other, to provide direct access to the West End and City for the great number of people who came to live around Ruislip and Greenford. At the same time the new line did much to relieve pressure on the Piccadilly Line.

To permit these extensions there were extensive alterations to the Central Line beyond Shepherd's Bush when Wood Lane station was abandoned and the new White City station, in the open and just to the west of it, took its place. Eastbound trains were enabled to pass one of the old Wood Lane platforms in the tunnel, but the westbound track detoured and avoided the old station altogether.

In 1949 the whole of the Wood Lane station area was being transformed, and Central Line trains were being stabled in part of the sheds built for the original Central London Railway rolling stock. The writer toured the area in that year to have a last look before the past vanished altogether. The old turntable that used to turn the heavy electric locomotives of bygone days was still in position, but rusted solid, one would imagine. Rearing overhead were the massive, peeling buildings of the Franco-British Exhibition that King Edward VII visited.

Beneath the forgotten Exhibition, in fact through its tremendous foundations, a new cut-and-cover tunnel had been driven. The old swing platform (mentioned earlier) and some of the tracks had been uprooted and laid aside, leaving half a station, some disused lines and a few forlorn notices about forgotten excursion trips to be read, perhaps, by the ghosts of those

Edwardians to whom the Exhibition was the latest wonder; they might easily have been imagined in this eerie place.

When Wood Lane was a terminal loop for Central Line trains, the tracks described an incredibly sharp curve to reverse the trains' direction; in consequence the old timber platforms of the station were bow-shaped. The writer had never before seen a platform so acutely curved, and certainly never again will see the like of all these remarkable Underground relics, for in 1963, London Transport partially concealed the past by building its new Training School on the site of the old tube's locomotive and car sheds. But the past was not completely obliterated, for a few years later he surveyed the scene from the new school's roof. In the background were the skeletal remains of the old Wood Lane station, and even some rusty ironwork of the old Exhibition. Most interesting were the faint outlines of the old reversing loop, still visible from above as a line of bare earth in the grassy space. The BBC Television Centre nearby now dominates the background, and in a few years all traces of the past may go if London Transport ever decides to house rolling stock elsewhere than in the old sheds still remaining.

The present westbound Central Line makes a wide sweep round the Wood Lane station site on its way to White City station. Between Wood Lane and North Acton there were, until 1938, only two tracks, and these were owned by the GWR, but Ealing tube trains used to operate over them, together with GWR steam-hauled goods trains. These two tracks obviously could not carry the additional traffic for the new extension, and the line was therefore quadrupled, so that the steam trains and later, diesel trains could keep to one pair of tracks, leaving the other for the Central's own exclusive use. The Central extension branches off the Ealing line just west of North Acton, and a burrowing junction was built so that westbound West Ruislip trains could diverge from the Ealing line without crossing its metals.

A point of interest about the new line is that no part of it had to be built in tunnel, although it is an extension of a tube railway. On the contrary, some of it is high above ground, on arches or on viaducts. Its tracks run alongside the former main line from Paddington to Birmingham and modern stations have replaced some of the old GW halts and stations.

There was, in fact, a striking contrast between the new and the old here. To see old halts alongside the splendid new stations was to realise how sparsely populated these districts must have been when the old steam service from Paddington to Ruislip & Ickenham was ample for all local needs.

An interesting feature at Greenford Station, which is built partly on a viaduct, is an escalator running from street level *up* to the platforms 30ft above, and this was the only instance where an escalator served such a purpose, until Alperton station acquired the feature. The platform arrangement at Greenford is unusual, for there is a central bay, almost dividing the island platform in two, which formerly accommodated Western Region steam trains made up of one tank locomotive and a coach working push-and-pull, running between Greenford and West Ealing, via the Castle Bar loop. It was hard to realise, in those days of multiple-unit tube railway stock, that this push-and-pull was the last relic of the trains which founded all the present extensive services. At all events, shortly after the writer last saw the steam train it was replaced by a diesel service to Ealing Broadway.

There was a considerable amount of constructional work needed on this portion of the line, for it had to be carried on a tremendously long succession of bridges and viaducts over roads, railways and waterways. There is a brick viaduct over the River Brent, between Hanger Lane and Perivale, followed by three long viaducts in concrete and several bridges or girder spans to carry the line over the east and west forks of the Western Region loop line to West Ealing.

Beyond Greenford the lines passes through South Ruislip, Northolt and Ruislip Gardens stations, and then over West End Lane by a plate girder bridge set very much on the skew — so much so that the girders have a maximum span of 99ft. Between Northolt and West Ruislip the main line and electric railways together occupy a great width of land, for the main lines widen to four tracks to the west of Northolt Junction, where the line from Marylebone joins that from Paddington. On the south side of the Central Line lies the extensive Ruislip Car Depot, 941ft long by 241ft wide, housing 16 tracks, each with its own inspection pit 440ft long. Including carriage sidings there are altogether 22 parallel lines of track here besides the running lines.

West Ruislip Station, the Central Line terminus, is a busy point, with two platforms for the main line services and an island platform for the Underground. At one time the main lines from Paddington constituted the major route to Birmingham via High Wycombe, but this ceased to be in 1967 when the major route was switched via Reading. (Even so, there is still a main line service through West Ruislip to Paddington, limited to one up and one down train per weekday — and of course the Marylebone passenger services, plus some freight traffic.) From this station the Central trains start on their 34½-mile through run to Epping; here, on one of the western outposts of the London Tranport railway system, one realises just how vast this system is. The Central Line tracks were built by the Great Western, and London Transport was given continuous running powers. After nationalisation, management and ownership were transferred in stages to London Transport; this process was completed in 1963.

It was on the eastern section of the Central Line, however, that the most comprehensive project was carried out. Southwest Essex, which had no tube railways before, possessed a splendidly long one when the big works were completed.

The grand scheme for the area affected included (a) electrification at 1,500V* of the LNER Colchester main line between Liverpool Street and Shenfield; and (b) the extension of the Central Line from Liverpool Street to connect with the LNER Loughton-Epping-Ongar branch and Grange Hill loop, which were to be electrified and resignalled.

The Central Line was extended, mainly in tube to connect with the District at Mile End and with the the LNER at Stratford. At Leyton the extension rises to the surface again, and continues above ground to Leytonstone. Here the route forks; some trains travel via Woodford to Epping, whilst others re-enter a new tube that brings them to the surface at Newbury Park, whence they travel once more in the open over the ex-LNER tracks to Hainault. Beyond Hainault the old steam line describes a curve and rejoins the Ongar line near Woodford.

The two loop services terminate at Hainault, one running as a shuttle service to and from Woodford, around the northern half, and the other using the southern half via Newbury Park to London. The six-mile stretch of line beyond Epping to Ongar was until November 1957 worked by steam trains, but the line has since been electrified throughout and is worked by a shuttle service of electric trains, as mentioned earlier. This stretch of single-track line has on more than one occasion faced complete closure for economic reasons. Following a Ministerial refusal of permission to close, London Transport decided to reduce the big gap between revenue receipts and overall expenditure by curtailing train services. As from the end of 1982 trains have operated only in a fairly wide band that covers morning and evening peaks, Monday to Friday. Blake Hall station, described as no more than a rural halt surrounded by farmland, closed in 1981, leaving only North Weald and Ongar beyond Epping.

The task of thrusting a tube through the waterlogged ground of the East London marshes might appear to the layman like a railway engineer's nightmare. Only the bare outlines of the work are described here, but the technical journals have given in matter-of-fact language a true detailed picture of this complicated undertaking.

Of one thing there is no doubt: there can be few finer examples in the world of successful tunnelling in the face of discouraging difficulties; and the result is a railway capable of providing for the travelling needs of many thousands who have to make the journey between London and the northeast suburbs. There are 9½ miles of double-track running line on this extension, 8½ miles of which are in tunnel, from Liverpool Street to Leyton, and from Leytonstone to Newbury Park. The extended tube runs from the Central Line platforms at Liverpool Street to a deep-level station at Bethnal Green, and afterwards rises to the level of the District Line at Mile End station. Then it dives again to deep level, continues for 1¾ miles without an intermediate station, and surfaces briefly at Stratford (Eastern Region) Station.

---

*This dc voltage was, under a British Railways' modernisation plan, converted to 25,000V (6,250V in places) ac.

At Mile End the tube rises to sub-surface through water-bearing ground. The compressed air method of boring could not be employed here because the depth of covering earth was insufficient, and the ground too porous to prevent air leakage. The problem was met by chemically treating the earth, both to consolidate it and hold back the water so that tunnelling could proceed. Some complicated work was also needed at the station, for the tube emerges on either side of the District tracks here, and the old station had to be transformed into a new one with double island-platform layout. Mile End is somewhat unusual as a tube station partly open to daylight (the west-bound platform) and consequently not in need of lifts or escalators.

Between Mile End and Stratford the line had to run beneath several streams that form part of the River Lea system. It was imperative to use compressed air under this marshy ground, and to provide sufficient ground cover the twin tubes were located beneath the LNER embankments. At river crossings, however, the embankment ceased, and the tubes were deprived of cover. Beneath the City Mill River only a few feet of waterlogged ballast lay between the tunnel shield and the bed of the river. A 'blow' here would have resulted in disaster, so the ground had again to be chemically consolidated, the injection pipes for forcing the chemical into the ground being driven from pontoons anchored in the river.

Beneath the Carpenter's Road LNER bridge, west of Stratford Station, it was impossible to use compressed air, because at this point the tubes are rising to the level of the main line, and lie only a little way below the road surface. Here it was necessary to sink two cofferdams (a kind of watertight enclosure) and partly build the tubes within them. A portion of the tunnel under the roadway had to be made only 7ft diameter to start with, owing to the presence of a larger sewer, but later, when diversion of the sewer became practicable, the tunnel was enlarged to 12ft.

The tube continues east of Stratford about 35ft below ground, until it rises in an open cutting to the site at the junction with the ex-LNER tracks west of Leyton Station. The eastbound tunnel runs directly beneath Loughton branch signalbox, and only 4ft of ballast lies between the tunnel top and the signalbox foundations. It was not practicable to build another signalbox on a fresh site, but chemical consolidation of the earth effectively preserved the brick foundations under the old box. The injection pipes were this time driven inside the cabin, right amongst the signal lever mechanism, and this was done without interruption to traffic.

If these complex projects were not sufficient to make this line unique, then wartime events might be thought to do so: as when in 1941 a bomb falling at Bank Station collapsed the entire roadway above into the subway. The resultant huge crater had to be bridged by the army, and closed the station for three months. Or when the nearly-finished tunnels of the extension were used as an underground extension to the Plessey Company's factory at Ilford, for the production of bomber and fighter plane parts. The wells of each tunnel were filled to make level floor space for machines, which were served by miles of light railway. Thus in 1940 these tunnels became one colossal factory, stretching from Leytonstone to Gants Hill, some 2½ miles. It had three stations, along its course: Wanstead, Redbridge and Gants Hill.

The factory was therefore nearly five miles long, since both of the 12ft diameter tunnels were utilised, and so that no employee should have to walk more than a quarter-of-a-mile to his (or rather *her*) machine, two intermediate points of entry were made in addition to the three stations, and lifts and escalators were installed. When it was decided to resume work on the tube railway extension, the colossal job of removing nearly five miles of concrete false floor had to be undertaken, so as to expose the normal track bed.

Some time after the new line was opened as far as Hainault, the writer went that far, stopping at the new and reconstructed stations on the Hainault Loop. The line is mostly in deep tube from Leytonstone to Newbury Park, having dived under the River Roding *en route*. Next to Newbury Park Station was a newish bus station, shaped like an arched hangar and entirely roofed with copper (which at today's prices sets one thinking of the golden roofs of Indian temples). On then to Barkingside and Fairlop stations at surface and embankment levels, where in its early years the line skirted a vast deserted airfield used during World War II by fighter aircraft, and subsequently built over. Then to Hainault, terminus for both north and south loop trains, with the lines fanning out to a large car depot housing 344 cars. Here, as at Ruislip, a train can be washed, wiped and buffed in the time it requires to crawl past the cleaning apparatus at 4mph.

The line here is about 20ft above road level, and beyond Hainault it curves left to Grange Hill, Chigwell and Roding Valley, after which it rejoins the Ongar line between Buckhurst Hill and Woodford. The surroundings when seen on that occasion were still rural, and the stations typical of their setting. The writer remarked on a tunnel mouth surmounted by a haystack, and a trial train disappearing within, with much sparking from the newly electrified track, that pleasantly contrasted with cattle munching in the fields. The advent of electric trains on the Woodford line necessarily closed several busy level-crossings, and at Snakes Lane a main road was severed, much to the indignation of local motorists. However, in several places where level-crossings were abolished, new road bridges were available near at hand.

This penetration of tube lines into southwest Essex did much to open up country still rural, whose travel needs were small and adequately met for many years by leisurely one-time Great Eastern Railway steam trains. These parts too are rich is history. Just along the road from Theydon Bois, next station to Epping, is Ambesbury Bank, where Boadicea, Queen of the Iceni, allegedly fought her last disastrous battle with the Romans. (Where today you are more likely to see a commuter's umbrella than a weapon of war.)

It will be realised that the Central Line extensions both east and west converge through Central London on to the two tracks of the original route, which had to be considerably altered to enable standard tube stock to be run. In the first place, the old three-rail system was converted to four-rail arrangement (that is, one incorporating a separate rail for current to return), and at the same time, the track rails were renewed and laid on transverse sleepers. In order to give the required clearances it was necessary to install the positive (outside) conductor rail slightly higher than in the standard position. This in turn necessitated a small modification to the current collector shoes of the Central Line rolling stock. Finally, the old stations were lengthened to 427ft to take eight-car trains.

On a level line these alterations could have been carried out by encircling the running tunnel with large sections of station tunnel. But, as we have seen, the Central track was originally constructed to enter and leave each station respectively on rising gradients, and falling gradients. Therefore, as the new sections of platform could not be sloped off, the nearer portion of each gradient had to be brought level, which meant steepening the remainder of each slope, sometimes by as much as 3ft to gain the extended platforms. The work took two years to complete, for, although it was attacked at several places simultaneously, the trains had to run, and only the early morning hours were left free.

The original Central Line was thus adapted to carry the additional traffic to and from the east and west extensions, a total of some 200 to 300 trains daily, and the old non-peak service headway of four minutes on the inner London section reduced in consequence.

The Piccadilly Line has also been transformed in recent years. Many of its important stations have been rebuilt and all its signalling has been modernised — in fact, except for the tunnels, practically everything has been altered since it was opened 80 years ago. This transformation took place when the line was extended north and west. Work on the 7½-mile northern extension from Finsbury Park to Cockfosters started in 1930 and the new line opened in stages. When finally completed in 1933, the extension rid the area around Finsbury Park Station of perhaps the most chaotic travelling conditions ever experienced in a London district.

For 26 years Finsbury Park had been the terminus of the two tubes, the Piccadilly and the Great Northern & City, and tens of thousands of tube travellers had to change here to buses, trams and surface trains, or vice versa. The cause of this chaos can be traced back to a covenant in the agreement dated 1902 between the Great Northern Railway and the Great Northern, Piccadilly & Brompton Railway, whereby the latter was not to extend the tube beyond Finsbury Park. However, no one foresaw in those days that eventually some 30,000 passengers would be changing here every weekday, and finally it became urgent that the veto in the 1902 covenant should be waived, and this was done in 1925.

As can be expected of a line which runs partly in tube and partly across undulating country, the Cockfosters extension has several interesting features, both below and above ground. For four miles, from Finsbury Park to a point between Bounds Green and Arnos Grove, it runs in twin tunnels, driven beneath Seven Sisters Road to Manor House, where they swing north on a 15-chains radius curve (the sharpest on this line of otherwise easy curvature) and continue beneath Green Lanes to Bounds Green. The gradient falls all the way to Turnpike Lane, and then rises at an average slope of 1 in 60 to the summit at Enfield.

Where the tube emerges at Tewkesbury Road, the tunnel is enlarged to 16ft, and bell-mouthed to reduce the air pressure on trains entering at speed. Just after the line leaves the twin tunnel it is carried obliquely across the wide North Circular Road on a 175ft girder bridge, which is supported in the centre by two pairs of pillars. After this is passes over a long viaduct to reach Arnos Grove station, and then enters a half-mile tunnel wherein is Southgate station. Emerging, the line rises in a cutting and is carried by viaduct and embankment to Enfield West (now Oakwood) and Cockfosters terminus, between which a large car shed is situated at the lineside.

The tunnelling work proceeded at the rate of half-a-mile of twin tunnel per month, and was, of course, carried on at several places simultaneously. It was driven mostly through London clay, and pneumatically-operated shovels were used to remove the clay from the many and various-sized shields employed. Altogether over 50,000 tons of iron tunnel segments were used on this extension. Much of the work was difficult, and one particularly delicate operation involved strengthening the brick tunnel through which the New River flows at Bounds Green. Here it was necessary to insert an iron lining for a distance of 90ft and this tricky job was done without interfering with the flow of the stream.

The housing boom of the 1930s transformed great expanses of open country around London into street upon street of detached and semi-detached houses. This growth of housing was not confined to any particular area, but went on at a rapid pace wherever there was 'easy access to London'. As the country filled up in the northern districts of Southgate and beyond, so it did in places like Hounslow, Ealing and Harrow, and it was considered advisable to balance the working of the Piccadilly Line by extending it at each end — just as the Central extensions were balanced some years later.

The Piccadilly services were therefore projected to the west and northwest concurrently with their extension first to Arnos Gove and later to Enfield West, now Oakwood, and finally on 31 July 1933, to Cockfosters. The western extensions, however, involved not so much a breaking of fresh ground as the adaptation of existing lines. In 1932, the Piccadilly service was extended from Hammersmith to South Harrow, then to Northfields in 1933, and later the same year to Hounslow West. Finally, in October 1933, it was extended from South Harrow to Uxbridge.

The District tracks already extended through Hammersmith to Hounslow, and from Northfields onwards it was simply a matter of Piccadilly trains using the District Line. But the District tracks between Hammersmith and Turnham Green, on the way to Northfields, were far too busy to accommodate additional Piccadilly trains, plus a lesser number of Richmond trains, and this particular bottleneck therefore had to be by-passed.

The problem was overcome partly by constructing a new 'cut and cover' tunnel under Hammersmith Broadway to take two new tracks, and partly by reopening the disused Southern Railway viaduct, which paralleled the District tracks to Turnham Green. At Hammersmith Broadway operations involved the removal and reconstruction elsewhere of an underground public lavatory, but the biggest and most spectacular work was the complete rebuilding of Hammersmith station to take the new four-track layout.

The adaptation of the Southern Railway viaduct was somewhat complicated, because the eastbound District track had to burrow through its arches where the viaduct curves away from the main Underground line, but the viaduct served to provide a four-track road where it was needed. Beyond Turnham Green the District tracks were quadrupled through Acton Town to Northfields by widening bridges, embankments and cuttings, thereby permitting a fast and a slow-road running arrangement. Between Northfields and Boston Manor a car depot, similar to that at Cockfosters, was built, with access from the running lines via a flyover junction.

The Piccadilly tube tunnels come to the surface at Barons Court, Kensington, and project their tracks between those of the District. From there, through Hammersmith to just beyond Acton Town, Piccadilly trains keep to the inner tracks and leave the two outer tracks for District trains.

The Richmond (District) trains branch off near Turnham Green, and to avoid conflicting train paths the eastbound Richmond branch track burrows completely under the four main tracks before curving in to join the main line. At Acton Town the Piccadilly service to South Harrow and Uxbridge leaves the Hounslow line and bears off right to North Ealing, South Harrow and Uxbridge, its westbound track being carried clear over the Hounslow tracks. To reach Uxbridge, the Piccadilly works over the old District line to South Harrow, and thence over the Metropolitan via Rayners Lane. Therefore, the Piccadilly western extensions to Hounslow and Uxbridge use existing lines almost throughout.

These extension services proved a boon, since passengers from districts as far apart as Uxbridge and Hounslow reach the heart of the West End without a change of trains. Moreover, the northern suburbs are connected directly to those in the west, the 15-mile journey from Ealing to Wood Green, for instance, occupying 41 minutes.

The extra traffic thus brought in to Central London had to be accommodated, of course, by enlarging and improving the existing stations. Leicester Square, Dover Street (now Green Park), Hyde Park Corner and Knightsbridge were reconstructed in the same style as Piccadilly Circus Station, which meant that the booking hall was placed beneath the road surface, and several entrances were provided from adjacent streets. Incidentally, wartime use of Underground stations (already referred to) should not pass without reference to one that had the distinction of sheltering the most famous personage of that period — Winston Churchill, and his War Cabinet. Between Green Park and Hyde Park Corner stations at a depth of 63ft lies the disused Down Street station, closed to passengers in 1932. It provided safe, deep-level accommodation during the air-raid blitz period. Somewhat earlier, Holborn was made an interchange station by closing British Museum station, Central Line, and building new platforms 100 yards east at the Holborn (Piccadilly Line) site.

This was an interesting operation, as the new platform tunnels of the Central Line at Holborn had to be built around the running tunnels, so that until the running tunnel tubes were dismantled, the spectacle was here again provided of trains running in a tube within a tube. At the same time escalator tunnels had to be built to connect Central to the Piccadilly platforms, and to the surface booking hall. In the same works programme, several Inner London stations, both on the Piccadilly Line and others, were reconstructed and provided with escalators.

The extension of the Piccadilly Line and the great increase in the area served naturally resulted in more passengers and more trains to carry them. Two distinct services, to Hounslow and Uxbridge, now used the former Piccadilly Line, and together they amounted to as many as 40 trains an hour on each road, a figure later reduced to two trains every 3½ minutes. The signalling system, practically unaltered from what it was for 25 years past, had necessarily to be brought up to date, and extended by the addition of several new signals to assist in the rapid clearance of trains. As an instance of improved running, the journey from Hammersmith to Finsbury Park took 37 minutes when the line was opened in 1906, and now takes only 28 minutes.

On the four-track section in West London the signalling had to be completely redesigned to deal with both the District and Piccadilly services, and it was here that an interesting and novel safety device was installed to safeguard the Piccadilly tunnel approaches against out-of-gauge stock. District rolling stock cannot, of course, attempt to enter tube tunnels, but since the four tracks can be used in common, there *is* the possibility of an eastbound District train being inadvertently switched to the eastbound Piccadilly tunnel, with dire consequences.

The safety device installed between Hammersmith and Barons Court consists of three U-shaped glass tubes filled with mercury and poised over the track at such a height that Piccadilly cars can pass clear beneath them, but District cars cannot. Should they attempt to do so, the tubes would be smashed and the mercury thus released would break all the electrical circuits for the eastbound Piccadilly home signals at Barons Court, putting the signals to 'Danger'. The automatic train stop apparatus, later described, would simultaneously come into action and effectually prevent the offending train from proceeding any further towards the tunnel.

In 1924, the reconstructed C&SL was for the first time connected with another of London's tubes, and this momentous development foreshadowed the great modernisation that has since assumed large proportions. An early progress was the extension of the C&SL north from Euston to Camden Town, where it joined the Hampstead and Highgate lines at the already celebrated Camden Town junction, and later the southern limit was extended into virgin country at Morden. These extensions created what was then the world's longest tunnel, from Golders Green to Morden via Bank, 16miles 1,100yd. This was subsequently exceeded by the High Barnet branch extensions of the Northern Line, whose present tunnel from East Finchley to Morden totals 17 miles 528yd.

The five-mile extension bristled with difficulties, the chief of which perhaps were encountered whilst building Tooting Broadway Station. In the past, the village of Tooting was noted for its plentiful water supply, and the tube station site lay over a subterranean lake. The station and its approaches had to be built under compressed air conditions, work being first conducted from beneath air-locks in vertical working shafts, and then from behind horizontal air-locks in the sections of tunnel completed. Very few of the many passengers using Tooting Broadway Station today realise that their station was built in waterlogged sand, and partly over a subterranean lake.

Camden Town junction, where no fewer than eight tubes meet, has been described often, and for many years to come will be regarded as a remarkable piece of railway engineering. The various tunnels ride over or dive under one another in a remarkable fashion, and their layout is so arranged that trains running between Moorgate or Charing Cross (now Embankment) and Edgware or Barnet can proceed through the junction without fouling each other's lines. To contrive this layout the north and southbound station tunnels, on both the Edgware and Barnet lines, had to be positioned one above the other.

In 1926 a new tube was opened from Charing Cross, and thence under the Thames to join the City & South London at Kennington. This was an extension of the Hampstead and Highgate tube southwards, linking it to the older line, and in the meantime the former had been extended northwards to Edgware. With this link, the first part of the plan was complete. One could travel from the green fields of Edgware to the green fields of Morden (they were green then) all the way by tube — and in the same train. From Highgate it was the same, and on both lines there was a choice of two routes, either through the West End and Charing Cross, or via King's Cross and the City.

The above more or less brings us to the great 1935-40 expansion programme, except that in 1933 every London line mentioned in this book, with the exception of the Waterloo & City, passed under the control of one body, the London Passenger Transport Board. It was the formation of this Board that allowed the expansion programme to be embarked upon, for before then the separate and competitive transport undertakings did not feel inclined to risk their capital on such a vast scheme, even though they knew the improvements were overdue. With the passing of the London Passenger Transport Act in 1935, the LPTB obtained Government consent to raise the huge capital jointly with the LNER and GWR, and the public was thereby assured of a 'gilt-edged' investment. The amount they subscribed was no less than £40,000,000.

The Northern Line's share in the programme was impressive and here it is in outline:

Electrification of the LNER branch lines from Finsbury Park to Alexandra Palace, High Barnet and Edgware; doubling the Finchley to Edgware branch; improvements to stations and re-signalling.

Construction and electrification of connecting lines between the Northern City Line and those just mentioned, through Finsbury Park.

Re-signalling the Northern City Line, lowering platforms to standard tube train height and installation of standard current rails.

Extension of the Highgate Branch, Northern Line, to East Finchley with interchange facilities for the Alexandra Palace branch at Highgate Station; new tracks, sidings and station at Edgware.

New rolling stock for the new lines; improvements to Camden Town substation; Elstree extension and new car depot at Bushey Heath.

Such of this work as was completed has been in operation for years. The tube has been extended beyond Archway to Barnet and Mill Hill East. Highgate Station was completed, but all high level tracks have been removed as services on the formerly steam-operated lines have been withdrawn. At East Finchley the old order gave way to a fine station on modern lines, but its centre tracks give access to car sidings only, and not an alternative route to the city as once intended. Similarly electrification beyond Mill Hill East to Edgware was never completed.

It is truly said that the only static thing is change. Change in thought and ideals has completely altered all the plans hereabouts, and the ubiquitous motorcar will alter them again, it seems. So much so that a completely new tube extending from Finsbury Park to the north-east suburbs has evolved, in order partly to relieve the chaotic street congestion caused by the same motorcar, partly to relieve the overcrowded Piccadilly Line and also to provide a much needed underground service from those suburbs to the City, West End, and Victoria. But of this more later.

Reverting to the extension of the Highgate branch, Northern Line, one can visualise the complexity of this undertaking, due in the main to the tube, in a relatively short distance, being required to rise from low level to a distinctly high level. Archway was for many years a terminal station (known then as Highgate) and two dead-end siding tunnels projected north for a short distance. One was extended to form a reversing siding with cross-over connections, and the other was continued as the new northbound tube. This, with its new twin tunnel, rises at 1 in 50, following the uphill course of Archway Road to Highgate Station, but even this fairly steep gradient brings the tube no higher than 80ft below the ex-LNER Highgate Station, and long escalators connect with the booking hall excavated beneath the abandoned former LNER station platforms.

But the old LNER station was itself built in a deep cutting, and even the surface line plunged into tunnels at either end of the platforms. Archway Road, the principal access to the station, is 60ft higher than the surface line, and further escalators have been built up the steep slope of the cutting to reach it. Highgate deep-level station is thus unique, with one long escalator to reach from the tube to sub-surface, and another long escalator tunnel in the open air, to climb the side of the cutting — a total ascent of 140ft. Highgate tube station is very long, over 160yd, and was built to accommodate nine-car trains, but this project was abandoned before other stations on this line were correspondingly lengthened.

An interesting wartime item is worth mentioning here. In September 1940, when the air raids on London were becoming intense, Highgate tube station was officially adopted as an underground dormitory for shelterers. It had not

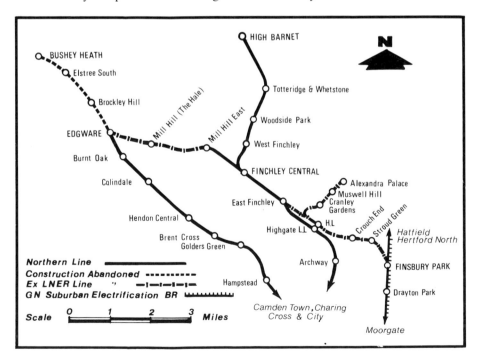

been opened for passengers because the escalators were not in position, and normally, no trains stopped there, but the Inner London stations became so overcrowded as shelters that special trains full of shelterers were run to Highgate and unloaded there. It was an unforgettable sight when travelling non-stop through this station, to see it brightly lit and crowded with sleeping people!

Beyond Highgate the tubes still rise, breaking surface one on each side of the ex-LNER tracks at East Finchley. All four tracks cross the Great North Road by bridge into East Finchley Station. At this point there was some difficulty with the levelling-off of the tube, for its exit had to be high enough for the line to cross the main road, and as far away from Highgate as possible in order to flatten out the gradient. This brought the exit rather close to East Finchley Station, and as a result the southbound track plunges rather abruptly, at 1 in 40, into a tunnel mouth that is slightly lower than its fellow. This drop was necessary as the southbound tunnel had to dive under the high level track here.

There was insufficient width of land at this point to enlarge the tunnel entry into the normal bell-mouth, and other means had to be found to minimise the air-pressure on trains entering the tunnel. It took the form of a number of pressure relief openings in the top of the tunnel, and these were strung out for some distance, gradually spacing out as they went. The need for this pressure relief can be understood when we realise that a tube train fits fairly snugly into its tunnel, and the effect of a train entering at speed is somewhat like that of a piston entering a cylinder. Were the sudden air-pressure not counteracted, passengers would experience an uncomfortable plugging sensation in the ears. Now, when a train drops into the Highgate tube at about 35mph, the air ahead escapes rapidly through the 'early' series of vents, and less rapidly as the vents string out as the train goes deeper into the tunnel; so that instead of a rapid increase, the air pressure builds up gradually.

North of East Finchley the lines converge on two tracks for the long straight run to Finchley Central. Finchley Central Station was to have been an imposing structure with two island platforms serving four tracks, but in view of the abandonment of the Bushey Heath extension no work took place. The Barnet tracks curve to the right here through a cutting, to continue for about four miles to High Barnet terminus, where there are car sidings. The Edgware track — which carried straight on — was in fact doubled according to programme, but the new set of rails disappeared during the war, leaving only a single electrified track to Mill Hill East, and a non-electrified track beyond.

From Finchley to Mill Hill East is quite a short but interesting run, for the line crosses a watered and well preserved parkland by a very high arched, brick viaduct, erected by the GNR for the Edgware branch (opened February, 1867) which the tube trains occupy as far as Mill Hill East, their present terminus. The writer has vivid memories of detraining at Finchley Central, and continuing his homeward journey to Mill Hill by bus under violent anti-aircraft barrage during the winter of 1940-41, and was grateful when the Mill Hill East branch opened in 1941, minimising the period of exposure to falling shell splinters.

Until the non-electrified track beyond Mill Hill East was lifted in 1964 and all rail traffic ceased, Eastern Region freight was the only traffic using the line between Mill Hill East and Edgware. This was the line destined to be electrified and doubled, with an entirely new railway branching off through a reconstructed Edgware Station and continuing for 2¾ miles to Elstree and Bushey Heath. The job was started, and earthworks and brick bases for viaduct arches were constructed, but there it finished, and as buildings have since been erected on part of the route, this project will never be revived. In fact the car shed, which was built near the proposed Bushey Heath terminus, is now incorporated in the London Transport Aldenham bus overhaul works, and was used during the war as an aircraft factory.

Although this part of the 1935-40 programme is as dead as the dodo, it may be interesting to the reader who might have seen over a period of years the massive steel skeleton structure at Finsbury Park and wondered why it was built, to do a little explaining. The structure was to have supported a new bridge across Seven Sisters Road and a new high level platform. This was to have been part of the physical link between the Northern City Line and the Alexandra Palace line.

At Drayton Park where the City Line is in the open, but at a depth of about 40ft, new running lines were constructed, leaving the old just north of the station in a cut-and-cover tunnel. They then emerge through trough-shaped cuttings to the surface, and were to continue to rise and be carried over a road overbridge to an island high-level platform at Finsbury Park. Thence the former flyover curve partly crossing the Eastern Region main tracks was to have been adapted to carry the tube across all the main tracks, on its way to the dizzy heights of Alexandra Palace station, an integral part of the Palace itself. But on 3 July 1954 the steam-operated passenger service was finally withdrawn. The district served by the line is well enough served, it seems, by other forms of transport; and even if electrified and connected to the City and West End, this short branch line was unlikely, in the light of present trends, ever to have justified the expenditure.

We mentioned earlier a project, the Great Northern Suburban Electrification Scheme, which entailed the transference and control of the Great Northern & City Line from London Transport to British Rail. This project partly reached fruition in 1976, when BR's new electrified trains began running between Welwyn Garden City, Hertford North and Moorgate via Finsbury Park and the old GN & City tunnel tracks. Thus no less than 73 years after the proposal was first made in 1903 to electrify the GN Suburban railway system, such suburban trains, of main line stock dimensions, began scheduled services through the very tunnels designed to take them all those long years ago.

We trespass on British Rail by any further comment on this project, but may be excused in so far as it is part of this line's history. Electrification of the surface stretches of the BR suburban network called for power collection by pantograph from overhead wires at 25,000V ac. The roof clearance of the old 'tube' section was however insufficient for pantograph collection, so this tunnel section is powered at 750V dc via a conductor track rail. The trains simply lower the pantographs, and collector shoes take over whilst standing at Drayton Park, and the procedure is reversed when leaving. And of course, all manner of work had to be carried out at the old GN & City underground stations to fit them in with the new rolling stock. (The massive steel structure at Finsbury Park, incidentally, was pulled down as it no longer had a purpose. The electrified tracks from Moorgate already were aligned to join the BR main line at Finsbury Park on the level, and did so by means of an existing rising junction and a new descending link-up.)

Right:
Freight traffic on the
Metropolitan was taken over in
1925 by the K class 2-6-4Ts.
No 113 was one of a batch built
to haul goods trains north of
Finchley Road. *LRT*

Below:
Underground stations were used
as air raid shelters during World
War II. Piccadilly Circus
platforms were photographed in
1940. *LRT*

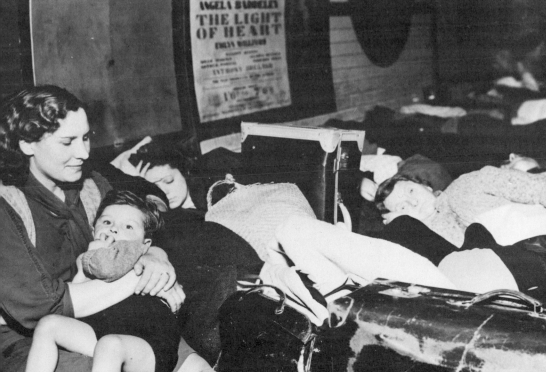

4
Development of the Underground Train

If the question were asked 'What is the special attraction of railways?' the answer would almost certainly be 'Their locomotives and rolling stock'.

There is something about a railway train that compels attention and the faster the train, the more it attracts, so perhaps the secret lies in its smooth, purposeful progress. Inevitably one's eye is turned to the locomotive, personifying harnessed power (more especially when it was steam), and the mind receives an impression of something majestic, important and swift, before whose rapid flight, paths must be cleared.

Electricity and the diesel engine have largely robbed us of this spectacle, and substituted something coldly efficient. A few of us may regret that the steam locomotive has become almost a thing of the past in this country — until we want to make a short railway journey in a hurry: and because several millions of us *have* to make short railway journeys every day, we know in our hearts that the electric train is a boon and a blessing.

To Londoners in particular the tube and sub-surface electric train has become a familiar object. Many people see it merely emerging from one tunnel and disappearing into another — in fact there must be lots of tube-travelling folk who never see the wheels of a tube train from one year's end to another, and if some of the cars moved on skids they would be none the wiser.

Part of the wonder, in fact, of this vast, partly subterranean railway system is that it is accepted so easily into the scheme of things. On the most heavily taxed sections of line, trains appear almost with the regularity of moving targets on a rifle range. The efficiency of the system naturally depends to a great extent on its rolling stock, which has developed since the early days of underground travel into a highly specialised type of vehicle. It continues to improve with each class of rolling stock delivered, and finality is fortunately never reached, because the car design which seems the last word today can always be bettered tomorrow.

We left the development of the multiple-unit train at a point where the early electric locomotives of the Central London Railway had been superseded by the motored carriage or car. That railway, tardily profiting by the example of the Waterloo & City Railway, made rapid strides when it substituted a motored bogie housing two 100hp motors for the plain bogie of an ordinary carriage and then completed the transformation by partitioning off the front end of this ordinary carriage so as to contain a driver's cab and switch apparatus.

The Central London trains, with a motored bogie at each end, were operated by multiple-unit controls so that, no matter how long the train was, the driver could control all its motors from his 'master controller'. The weight of one of the early types of motorcoach, with its fireproof-lined switch compartment, all the apparatus, and a full complement of passengers, was about 23½ tons.

Roughly at the same time as the Central was experimenting with different forms of traction, that is, in the early 1900s, the Metropolitan and District Railways were also experimenting with new trains for their electrification scheme. Following the initial tests of steam versus electricity at Earl's Court, two seven-car trains of the open saloon type, seating an average of 46 passengers per car, were run on the 5½-mile length of District track between Acton Town (then known as Mill Hill Park) and South Harrow. They were, of course, larger and heavier than the Central tube stock, being built to main line loading gauge, and their motor-cars, three to a train, were powered with 175hp motors; a maximum speed of 60mph was claimed. They were fitted with hand-operated sliding doors in the middle, and gates at each end platform. What was known as 'turret' control was installed, and its circular grouping of the contacts effected a great saving in weight and space.

Generally speaking, it can be said that the electric trains of the Metropolitan, the District, the Metropolitan & Great Western Joint (whose line extended from Hammersmith to Edgware Road) and the Great Northern & City Railways were all composed of coaches built to the same generous scale, which allowed for a coach body over 8ft high, nearly 9ft wide, and approximately 12ft high, overall, above rail level. There was sufficient space for equipment to be placed beneath the car floors without the latter having to be raised in any part, and thus detract from the space available for passengers.

The Metropolitan and District Railways' electric rolling stock had certain similarities, but the early District car, with its angular appearance and open end platforms, resembled more the old American observation car that one occasionally sees on the cinema screen. This was not to be wondered at, considering that an American not only dictated the design, but actually supervised construction of the stock at Loughborough. The design of these cars was in fact pretty conclusively American, for although this country was the first to operate electric railways, rapid transit by electrically operated railways was, by the early 1900s, being developed extensively in America. Railway concerns in that country were already considering means to avoid delays caused by the loading and unloading of passengers from overcrowded cars by means of end doors only, with the result that a new design of car was introduced in Boston, with a door in the centre as well as doors at the ends. It was this type of car which was adopted by American engineers on the Metropolitan District Railway in London.

There was an experiment in those early days to operate the sliding doors on District cars by pneumatic pressure, but it was found too costly and otherwise unsatisfactory, and the doors were altered from pneumatic to manual operation. Fully automatic door operation was, however, to come on this line, as on other railways, but it had to wait many years before it could be considered absolutely safe and efficient.

The old types of car were certainly decorative, as befitted the age. Those of the District, for instance, had heavy plate glass windows with brilliant-cut decorations, and an interior finished in polished mahogany with white ceilings decorated with gold. The exteriors were painted vermilion. Again, the Metropolitan Railway's coaches were most handsome, with their varnished teak sides and colourful coats of arms. But the lavishness of those times would appear out of place in this streamlined age, as would first and third class accommodation on Underground trains — and it is a wonder that this distinction persisted as long as it did. On the Metropolitan and District Railways first class did not disappear until 1942.

The rolling stock of the Metropolitan had for many, many years been divided into 'main line' and 'local', the former including that working to Uxbridge, Watford, Rickmansworth and beyond, whilst the New Cross, Shoreditch trains were local: but this cannot be regarded as a rigid demarcation,

On the tube railways the first cars of the City & South London, the Central, and later the Hampstead and other lines were squat and rounded, designed to negotiate circular tunnels affording only a limited head room. These tunnels allowed for a maximum car-body height of just over 7ft and a total height above rail level of about 9ft 6in. Each company's stock differed in appearance, but the common limitations of a narrow tube kept their outlines similar. As with the Metropolitan and District stock, streamlining and total enclosing have altered the appearance of later types of deep level stock; but the most noticeable difference, for those with long memories, is the disappearance of the end platforms, the gates, and the gatemen who operated them.

The robustness of the earlier stock, however, is well illustrated by the fact that two tube cars, part of the original fleet which opened the Great Northern, Piccadilly & Brompton Railway in 1906, were in use no less than 50 years, finishing their passenger service careers on the Holborn-Aldwych shuttle service. They were converted to air-door operation after World War I, and, in 1930, re-converted to work as single shuttle cars on the Aldwych branch. They owed their long life to a service break of five years when the line was closed and used as an air raid shelter during the last war, and were finally used as driving cars for stores trains between Acton Works and Northfields Depot.

One of the driving motor-cars of the 1920s has been preserved. No 3327, repainted and reconditioned, with nearly 1½ million running miles to its credit, went on exhibition alongside a section of platform representing part of a London Underground station in the Science Museum, South Kensington, London. To many millions of contemporary Londoners who were carried to work and home again on those sturdy old vehicles it may conjure up nostalgic memories.

The Piccadilly extensions northward and westward changed conditions on that line and demanded faster trains with increased capacity, which was largely met by operating seven-car trains with three motor-cars as against six-car trains with two motor-cars.

The weight of the new cars was kept at a minimum by using aluminium alloy wherever possible and by building the steel structure of light pressings. External surfaces of the coachwork were rounded off to permit a smoother passage through the car washing apparatus. Inside re-arrangement resulted in the guard's control panels in motor-cars being built into the end walls, and the addition of power-operated single-leaf doors at each end.

The motor-cars on these trains, like all other 'pre-1938' stock motor-cars, had a bulky switch compartment placed over the motor bogie. It was advantageous to the fitter, who could inspect the equipment from both inside the compartment and also from outside, by raising louvres in the coachwork. The disadvantage of passenger space lost to the switch compartment, however, marked these cars as obsolescent and they gave way to the type that carries all its main equipment below floor level.

It can be imagined that the multiple-unit train, with its control positions all interconnected, contains much complicated apparatus. Most of this is concerned with the functioning of traction motors, brakes and air-operated doors, and irrespective of where the apparatus is housed, its operation, so far as the brake and motor equipment is concerned, is similar on the majority of trains.

But the reader need not imagine the driver as having to cope with a mass of relays, cut-outs or resistances. Just as the driver of a steam locomotive had an ultimate control in the regulator, so the driver of an electric train is only concerned with a single controller handle, and his judgement is transmitted through cables to switch devices, which in turn control the electric current fed to several powerful motors spaced throughout the train. The various devices obey the driver or the guard unquestioningly, thereby leaving these men free to devote all their attention to the working of the scheduled service.

What happens when a driver operates his master controller is this:

Contactors or switches, operated electro-pneumatically, connect the motors to the current supply, at first in series through starting resistances wherein surplus electrical energy, which motors running at slow initial speed cannot 'assimilate', is allowed to waste in the form of heat. As the train gathers speed an accelerating relay cuts out the starting resistance in a number of steps by the automatic closing of contactors, or switches if you like. When all the resistance has been cut, each motor is working on only half the voltage of the power supply, but is sufficiently accelerated to start absorbing the full line voltage. The next phase is therefore the re-grouping of the motor circuits in parallel, with the starting resistances again in operation. They are cut out in steps as before, until finally the motors are in full parallel; that is, they are receiving the full voltage, being connected directly across the power supply. In the improved type of control, the more sensitive rapid pneumatic accelerator, basically a small air-oil engine operating contacts, replaces the old individual contactors. The stages are as before, but at the intermediate stage a valve operating on the engine forces air against oil, which in turn moves a piston and camshaft and cuts out resistances. The third, parallel, stage is reached with resistance automatically restored, but at this point the engine operates in reverse and allows the motors full voltage by cutting out resistances. It should be appreciated that these movements, although appearing lengthy and involved, take place in the few seconds that the train is getting under way.

In the event of an interruption to the source of power supply, a 'no volt' relay in the circuit comes into operation. Its purpose is to prevent the full voltage being suddenly fed to the motors after such an interruption, by ensuring that the equipment is returned to its original starting condition, with the complete sequence of operations to follow. The driver may move his controller freely through several accelerating positions, or notches, but the accelerating relay automatically ensures that the proper sequence is traversed. Should he lift his hand off the controller handle, the main supply to the controller is broken, current is cut off, and the brakes are applied. This is a safety device fitted to all London Transport rolling stock to safeguard the train from a driver's personal mishap, such as illness or collapse. Tersely but somewhat grimly, this safety cut-off is called the 'dead man's handle'.

Before concluding these remarks on traction motor control, mention should be made of apparatus presently undergoing test known as thyristor control. It is also referred to as chopper control because its action in regulating current employs a chopper movement. Very basically the thyristor can be likened to an electronic one-way valve providing an instantaneous current limiter. In this case the control smooths acceleration and reduces electrical losses throughout that function. Also, the kinetic energy of a train during braking is (more importantly) converted back into electric current, available for use by other trains during their acceleration: but only when such trains are in the same electrical section as that regenerating the current, since electricity cannot be stored. This form of traction motor control is likely to be extended initially on Central Line trains.

The 1935-40 new works and improvements programme added many miles to the London Transport system, and included provision for much new rolling stock, the total number quoted being 1,694, of which 573 were intended for surface lines and 1,121 for deep level tubes. The surface line stock was built by the Gloucester Railway Carriage & Wagon Company, and the Birmingham Railway Carriage & Wagon Company.

All the surface stock trains built under these orders have now been withdrawn from service, and the few remaining tube stock trains were not expected to survive beyond 1986.

Designed to replace the early District and Metropolitan saloon stock, cars of O, P and Q stock entered service between 1937 and 1939. Their elliptical roofs, flush fitting windows and flared body panels gave the cars an extremely sleek appearance. All doors were air-operated under the guard's control; with O stock the controls were in the cab, but with P stock in the passenger saloon. These cars were for the Metropolitan and the couplers were made automatic, but for the District Q stock, couplings were made to suit existing cars. The O and P cars, later known as CO and CP when fitted with BTH PCM control equipment, were the last red painted surface trains, and were withdrawn in 1981.

The District R stock trains survived until 1983, and consisted of converted Q cars and other visually similar postwar builds. There were no trailers, and every car was fitted with a 110hp motor in each of its bogies. Later batches had aluminium bodies some six tons lighter than their steel counterparts, and the earlier cars were painted silver to match. One of the cars in the final R59 batch was sent to an international exhibition at Strasbourg in June 1960, the first time that a London Underground car had been sent abroad, although not the first time that such a vehicle had made a Channel crossing. Many of the original tube cars were built on the Continent. Delivery of the R stock trains made possible the scrapping of early District steel cars and Circle Line wooden cars in 1950-1.

There are three types of surface stock in use today. 248 aluminium bodied saloon type cars were delivered by Cravens Ltd in 1961 for the newly electrified services to Amersham and Chesham. They are unusual for Underground cars, having high-backed transverse seating only, with two and three seats each side of a central gangway. These replaced the remaining locomotive-hauled coaches, and also the electric compartment stock on the Watford line. A later delivery of 216 similar cars replaced earlier stock working on the Uxbridge line.

The performance of these trains, known as A stock, was arranged to conform with that of the stock then running over the same lines. In effect this means that the traction motors can be controlled to either a high or low acceleration rate suiting in-town density conditions, where the average station to station distance is ½-mile; or using a different acceleration rate together with a different motor-field strength, full advantage of the longer outer sections beyond Baker Street can be taken with operational speeds of 60mph.

The train's braking equipment includes the normal electro-pneumatic service brakes incorporating the standard London Transport form of retardation control.

This form of retardation control obviates over-fierce braking effects and comprises essentially two tubular rings of glass containing mercury, so mounted that when a certain pressure of braking has been reached the mercury flows up one of the tubes and indirectly cuts off further supplies of air to the brake cylinder. Should the braking approach a severity sufficient to lock the wheels, the forward surge of the train causes a similar displacement of mercury in the second tube which releases air from the brake cylinder, and eases the brake shoes off the wheels, thus allowing a train to be braked evenly and smoothly to a standstill.

These trains are presently undergoing modifications, which include the resiting of the guard's control panels to the driving cabs to make the stock suitable for one person operation.

For the Hammersmith & City, Circle Line and Edgware Road-Wimbledon services new sub-surface C stock, comprising 46 six-car trains, was first ordered in 1968 from Metro-Cammell, and delivered in two batches during the 1970s. The trains differed from the A stock in so far as they were designed for urban or inner London traffic, and consequently shorter journeys with considerable movement in and out of trains. Among their new features was a secondary suspension system of rubber-air springing units, thermostat-controlled blower-heater fans mounted in the roofs, and extra doors whose vestibules afforded an increase in standing space but lessened the number of seats. This was the first manually controlled stock on London Transport to be fitted with a rheostatic brake — using the traction motors for braking. All these trains have now been modified to make them suitable for one person operation.

For the District Line proper, all aluminium D78 stock was introduced in stages from January 1980. The fleet of 75 D78 trains made up of two three-car units (driving motor-cars, trailers and driving or non-driving motor cars) are similar in length, about 363ft, to the seven-car trains they replaced. Important new features were single-leaf passenger operated doors (the guard closes them), and four doors on each side of each car. For safety reasons the push-button operation only works when the train guard illuminates a surrounding 'Press to open' sign. He can also re-open any door failing to close properly, and all doors in an emergency.

Seating is mainly longitudinal. In the trains' ceilings are concealed fans. These were boosted by additional fans after experience, and this measure coupled with the installation of opening quarterlights cured the trouble of excessive heat. The car wheels and motor bogies (each with two motors) are interchangeable with those on the Piccadilly Line trains. Traction brake controls were also new, comprising a right-hand 'fore and aft' vertical lever incorporating the 'dead-man' device, instead of the previous left-hand, rotary-operated controller. D78 trains can easily be converted to one person operation, which includes driver control of passenger doors. They were manufactured by Metro-Cammell of Birmingham

In the 1935-40 new rolling stock programme for the Tube lines, Metropolitan-Cammell built 644 driving motor cars and shared the construction of 206 non-driving motor cars with the Birmingham RC&W company, who also built 271 trailers. The chief aims of this stock, designated 1938, were increased passenger accommodation and a better standard of comfort, with improved performance.

As in the experimental sets constructed in 1935, all control and traction equipment was removed from its traditional home in a compartment behind the driver, to new positions beneath the floor, thus providing extra passenger space. The seating capacity of the motor cars was thereby increased from about 30 to 42 passengers, and an additional set of double doors each side permitted the reduction of waiting time for loading and unloading. The non-driving motor-car was a new departure. Here for the first time an effort was made to distribute motor power throughout the train for the sake of more rapid acceleration and higher speed.

Trains made up of this stock were divided into semi-permanently coupled units of three and four cars, each unit with a driving cab at either end. They featured the under-floor electrical equipment arrangement, and air-operated doors (as on the surface stock) safeguarded in that the guard's indicator lamp lights up only when all doors are closed properly, permitting him to give the starting signal. Also on the Metropolitan surface stock, automatic coupling makes possible an instantaneous connection of the mechanical,electrical and pneumatic mechanism as well as cutting out the trip-cock, no longer needed in what then becomes the middle of the train. In comparison with the older type of train, the total tractive effort became 1,680hp as against 1,440hp.

After the war, another new car type, the uncoupling non-driving motor-car was introduced as 1949 stock; these cars were equipped with simplified driving apparatus for shunting purposes only, and took the place of some inner-end conventional driving motor cars. Originally the 1938/49 cars monopolised services on the Bakerloo and Northern Lines, with 15 additional sets on the Piccadilly; the few that remained in 1985 operated on the Bakerloo.

On the tube lines, stock variations reflect the differing conditions on individual lines. Following construction of prototypes in 1956, the aluminium bodied car with rubber bogie bolster and axlebox suspension, fluorescent lighting, trackless doors and door fault indicator lights became standard. Mass produced as seven-car trains for (initially) the Piccadilly (1959 stock), and as eight-car trains for the Central (1962 stock), these cars otherwise followed closely the 1938 stock design. Their construction was shared between Metro-Cammell and British Railways' workshops at Derby. It had been intended to equip the Central Line with new stock based on the 1960

Cravens design, but in the event 12 motor cars only were constructed; the cars which survive have been converted to Automatic Train Operation (ATO), and ply between Woodford and Hainault.

The Victoria Line trains or 1967 stock, began running experimentally as far back as 1964 and were built for Automatic Train Operation (ATO) — described later. The trains, which are designed to suit mainly 'in-town' passenger traffic and therefore provide more room for standing passengers, are operated by one man. He closes the doors, presses the twin starter buttons, and from then on the acceleration, coasting, and braking to the next station are automatic. The train slows, stops and re-starts as required by the position of the train ahead, or to conform to any speed restriction. The operator can take over manually in the event of failure of the automatic equipment. The aluminium-alloy car bodies, on a steel underframe, have their driving ends protected by 'wrap-round' windscreens, without corner pillars. The car's primary springing is of the rubber type, as in all recent Underground stock, but the secondary suspension incorporates hydraulic suspension-control units.

Tractive power is provided by 80hp motors driving on all four axles of the driving motor-cars. A new form of braking combines two systems acting in three stages — rheostatic braking on motored wheels only, rheostatic braking on motored wheels and air braking on trailer wheels, and both rheostatic and air braking on motored wheels and air braking on trailer wheels, operating in conjunction with mercury retardation control.

Fitted headlights on trains can light the tunnel ahead to give the operator some idea of the train's movement in the absence of colour-light signals (of which there are few). Other features include internal loudspeakers for operator-to-passenger announcements and a carrier-wave telephone unit for communication between train operators and traffic control. (Rheostatic braking as referred to is defined as a method where motors are used as generators, dissipating energy in rheostats and thus exerting a retarding force.) These trains were built by Metro-Cammell, as were all the tube trains which followed up to and including the 1983 stock.

Similar in design and appearance, the 1972 Mk I stock for the Northern (30 trains) and the 1972 Mk II stock for the Jubilee and Northern Lines (33 trains) were built for crew operation. Trains of Mk II stock are visually distinguishable by their smart red painted doors. One of the Mk II driving motor cars took part in an overground procession in 1981, as it was exhibited in the Lord Mayor's show!

The 88 new trains of 1973 Tube stock delivered in the mid-1970s for the Piccadilly Line had to be designed to operate to and from Heathrow Airport (over the new extension from Hounslow West). To cater for airline passengers carrying baggage, extra floor space has been provided which can be used for standing passengers as well as the baggage. At the same time it had to be realised that baggage in any quantity moved off and on trains by the owners would cause delay in mid-town stations, where speed in discharging and embarking passengers is essential in order to maintain the intensified service demanded during peak hours. The additional space was made possible by setting back the glass screens at door openings to provide larger vestibules than normal. The car interiors are otherwise similar to those on the Victoria Line. Externally the individual cars are longer than normal. Made up into six-car trains, the total length of a new train is 350ft (107.6m), about 17ft (5.23m) less than the seven-car trains they have replaced. This train length was designed so as to be accommodated in existing below-ground stations, and also in accordance with a wish to provide for one-man operation, not possible on this line with seven-car trains of normal length.

Among advantages of the six-car train are fewer bogies per train (and consequently less cost), a saving in weight and noise, and a greater degree of comfort. The total passenger capacity in nevertheless about the same as in seven-car trains. It may be thought that with these advantages, London Transport might consider introducing these longer cars on other lines. But some passenger stations on other lines have their platforms built on a curve, where the longer cars would leave a gap between car and platform not consistent with safety.

This brings us to the most recently acquired Tube trains, those for the Jubilee Line, designated 1983 Tube stock. Similar to the Piccadilly's 1973 stock, a 1983 train is made up of two three-car units, differing from the 1973 stock in so far as it includes a modified ventilation system of seven roof-mounted extractor fans and new types of radiant heater (both thermostatically controlled), passenger-operated single-leaf doors as on the D78 stock, a driving cab fitted with train information display unit, two-way radio and public address systems. Fifteen trains have been built.

On the day that the 1983 stock trains entered service, 2 May 1984, it was announced that prototype trains for new Central Line stock had been ordered. The new stock is named 1990, in anticipation of its hoped-for date of introduction.

Metro-Cammell are building two of the four-car prototypes and the third will come from British Rail Engineering Ltd at Derby. Electrical equipment will be supplied variously by GEC-TPL of Manchester, Brown-Boveri of Zurich and Brush Electrical Machines Ltd of Loughborough. Each of the three trains will consist of two two-car units, with one car having a driving cab and the other no cab; they will be about 16m and 15.6m long respectively. The automatic coupling arrangements between units and the controls of all three trains are designed to be compatible so that any combination of two-car units can couple to form an eight-car train.

The main technical features to be tested on the prototypes are:

- Welded aluminium alloy bodies, including the floor structure
- External sliding doors
- Air suspension
- Dimpled rubber type floors
- All axles motored with chopper control to save energy, and to give smoother acceleration and braking
- Lightweight fully sprung motors to reduce vibration, or steerable bogies to reduce rail and wheel wear.
- Improved ventilation and heating.

Dot-matrix train destination indicators on the train front will be linked to similar indicators inside each end of every car. The interior indicators will normally show the destination but, as the train approaches each station, trackside equipment will change the display to name the next station and an audible signal will operate.

Passengers will have door-opening buttons mounted on the doors, and closing buttons for use at termini. There will be special tones to indicate when doors are about to close or may be opened. Three internal layouts are to be tried out, with substantially increased standing space compared with existing tube stock. The number of seats will thus vary from 32 to 42 per car.

The new trains will be fitted with automatic train operation apparatus and could conceivably become the first NOPO operated stock (ie operated without any staff on the trains) in London.

In view of the many changes of stock operating individual lines, due to replacement necessities, for instance (a process which has occupied many years), it has been decided to conclude this section on Underground train development with a list, which may serve as a rough guide for those readers interested in in identifying stock in service.

Use of underground rolling stock
Summer 1985

Surface Lines

A60/62   Metropolitan (Amersham, Uxbridge and Watford services): eight-car trains
Chesham branch shuttle: four-car train

C69/77   Circle, Metropolitan (Hammersmith & City service), District (Edgware Road-Wimbledon service): six-car trains

D78   District (Upminster-Ealing Broadway, Richmond and Wimbledon services): 6-car trains. Metropolitan (East London Line service): three-car trains

Tube Lines

1938	Bakerloo: seven-car trains
1956	Northern: seven car trains
1959	Northern, Bakerloo: seven-car trains
1960	Central (Woodford-Hainault branch): three-car trains
1962	Central: eight-car trains (and one four-car on Epping-Ongar branch); Northern: seven-car trains
1967	Victoria: eight-car trains
1972 Mk I	Northern: seven-car trains
1972 Mk II	Jubilee, Northern: seven-car trains
1973	Piccadilly: six-car trains (three-car trains on Aldwych and Central Line Woodford-Hainault branches)
1983	Jubilee: six-car trains

The 1983 Tube stock is still being delivered to the Jubilee Line, enabling 1972 Mk II trains to be transferred progressively to the Northern Line. This, in turn, allows more 1959 Tube stock to be transferred to the Bakerloo to replace the 1938 Tube stock, which is being scrapped. On completion, the Bakerloo will be equipped with 1959 Tube stock, the Jubilee will have 1972 Mk II and 1983 stock, and the Northern will have 1956, 1959, 1972 Mk I and 1972 Mk II Tube stock.

During 1985 a specially renovated train of 1938 Tube stock may be seen in service on the Bakerloo Line. It has been restored as far as possible to its original condition and in 'train red' livery rather than the 'bus red' used in recent years. It is made up of a four-car unit and a three-car unit, although these may be allocated to different trains if need arises. It is intended that it will subsequently be preserved in working order.

London Transport ceased its steam passenger train operation in 1961, but maintained some Metropolitan steam locomotives until these too were replaced by ex-Western Region BR pannier tank locomotives. Finally these too were replaced by diesel-hydraulic locomotives in 1971 for shunting, and additional battery locomotives for line duties.

A veteran Metropolitan steam locomotive, L45, built in 1866, is preserved in the London Transport Museum at Covent Garden, London. Until 1905, this old locomotive hauled passenger trains on the Inner Circle Line, subsequently being used for less onerous duties by the Metropolitan Railway, and finally it was demoted to London Transport service use. But fittingly it is now restored to its 1903 condition and livery and has been given its original number — 23.

There are also a number of battery-driven locomotives that operate wherever possible on current obtained from the conductor rail, during which time the batteries are recharged in readiness for use where no live supply exists. They are fitted with very prominent buffers, which are hinged at the top, so that when necessary the buffers may be swung right up out of the way to permit close-coupling through the central automatic couplers. Some were used on the Victoria Line and the Piccadilly Line for the extension to Heathrow Central, and some were in use on the Jubilee Line construction works. Six new improved locomotives were acquired in 1983-4.

Then there were the 'sleet' locomotives, which helped to solve the problem of current collection from conductor rails coated with frost, snow and ice. Devices known as 'de-icing baths' — now largely replaced by equipment and fluid carried on a proportion of passenger trains — are built into the conductor rails on open sections, and contain anti-freezing solution which the collector shoes pick up and distribute: but to break up hard ice and get the rails into usable condition needs a more positive attack. The 'sleet' locomotives attacked the conductor rails with anti-freeze solution, liquid sprayers, and wire brushes, and certainly helped to keep the lines open in very bad weather. Compressed air actuated the valves controlling the de-icing fluid, and by operating cylinders using the same medium, the brushes and ice-cutting rollers were lowered to the rails to do their work, the compressed air for all functions being obtained from battery-operated electric pumps.

Included in the impressively large total of London Transport's miscellaneous rolling stock are ballast motor-cars, diesel-electric cranes, rail grinding cars, ballast, flat and hopper wagons, and a unique five-car train designed to dislodge dirt and dust and collect it, from Tube tunnel walls.

It is not unusual to find service cars that have had their day being converted for other less spectacular but useful duties, and such has been the case with two 1923 class Central Line cars. Whilst their fellows went for scrap these two underwent almost a metamorphosis and emerged as rail grinding cars, replacing two even earlier specimens. To these are fitted aluminium-oxide blocks mounted in shoes on their bogies. The cars' inside space, once filled with seats and the like, now holds water tanks. The coupled cars are themselves coupled fore and aft to motor-cars when work is required of them, and the strange train takes to the tracks during non-service hours and makes its way to a worn stretch of line needing a little treatment. Arriving there, it works to and fro at around 30mph with nozzles spraying water on the blocks as, forced down on the running rails by pneumatic pressure against spring back-resistance, they steadily grind away corrugations, doing their small part act in making journeys just that much less noisy. These cars are currently stored.

Travelling diesel-electric jib cranes, each with a 37ft long swan-neck jib, are enabled to negotiate curves in tunnels as the jib foot becomes automatically articulated when the jib is lowered to its carrier wagon. The maker, Taylor &

Hubbard Ltd, used considerable ingenuity in producing a crane capable of lifting 5½ tons at 15ft radius free on rail, or 6 tons at 16ft radius blocked up, which clears cable posts, platforms, etc, when towed at service speeds and can thus quickly reach any site on the Underground network.

And finally there are the hopper ballast wagons and the long flat wagons built of welded steel sections that slip out of depots, usually at the dead of night, loaded with material to make good the 'way and works'. We can imagine these service trains and their crews, the permanent way men and signal staff, returning in the early morning to a well-earned rest, with the knowledge that the line is restored to condition in readiness to bear the brunt of another hard day's running.

Right:
City & South London Railway original electric locomotive, today preserved in the Science Museum, South Kensington. 52 were eventually built, each weighing between 10 and 14 tons; they were expected to haul three trailers in service.
John Glover

Below:
After a disastrous flirtation with locomotives, the Central London Railway opted for multiple-unit traction. One of the new motor cars is seen with the original trailers at Wood Lane depot.
LRT

Left:
The 1898 shunting locomotive No 75S was used in the sidings at Waterloo to shunt stock until 1968, when it was retired to the National Railway Museum. It was photographed at York in 1983 in chocolate livery. *John Glover*

Below left:
Steam locomotive No 27, one of the 66 4-4-OTs used by the Metropolitan Railway and built by Beyer Peacock between 1864 and 1885. No 23 is preserved in the London Transport Museum. *LRT*

Below:
The exterior of one of the trailers, the famous padded cells. Access was by an open platform and a door at each end only. *LRT*

Right:
Interior view of a padded cell car. The wooden bodies were a mere 26ft long, 6ft 10in wide and 7ft high. Reputedly, 60 passengers could squeeze into them. *LRT*

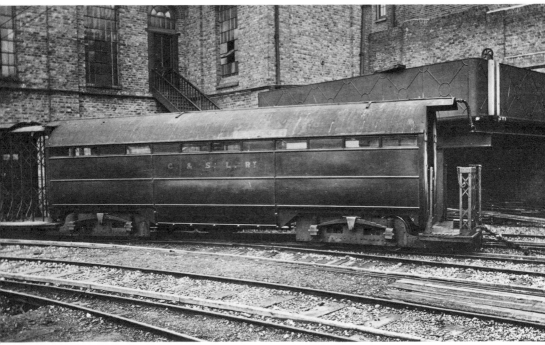

Left:
Early booking offices were entirely manual, with dexterity by the clerk relied on to cope with lengthening queues. This is Golders Green office in 1912. *LRT*

Right:
The car interiors were much superior to the offerings on the CSLR. In this CLR trailer, there are large windows, rattan seating and stuffed armrests. See p77 for external view. *LRT*

Below right:
The motor car of an experimental District train first tried out in 1903 between Mill Hill Park (the present Acton Town) and South Harrow. *LRT*

Below:
At South Kensington, the tube and surface railways had their station buildings alongside each other, although the stations were not fully integrated until the 1970s. The contrast in styles is evident, with decorative ironwork on the one and shiny red bricks on the other. *John Glover*

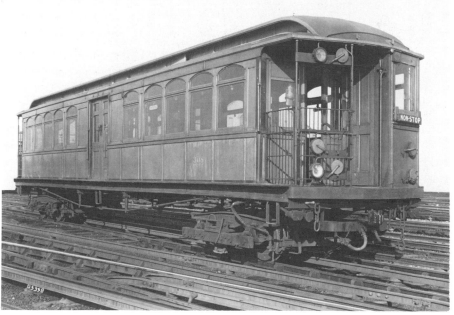

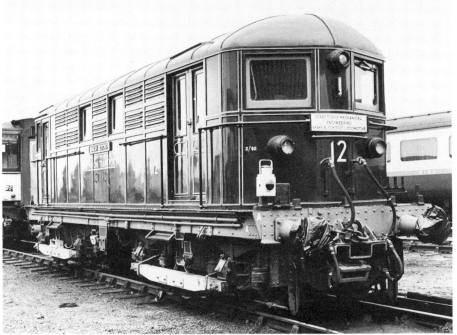

Left:
Instruction train for the staff of the Chief Mechanical Engineer (Railways) formed of five trailer cars of a batch of the 40 supplied by Cammell-Laird for the Bakerloo Line in 1919. *LRT*

Below left:
Sarah Siddons, No 12 of the Metropolitan Railway's electric locomotives used on the Rickmansworth services until 1960, is the only one to remain in working order. She is seen here at Eastleigh on public exhibition in 1983. *John Glover*

Right:
Q stock car No 4248 today resides in the London Transport Museum, representing a typical clerestory roofed vehicle. It dates from 1923. *John Glover*

Below:
A 5-car Metropolitan Circle Line train displays its prominent indicator boards around 1920. *LRT*

Left:
1927 built Standard Stock
Driving Motor Car No 3327 has
had cab door and bodyside
ventilators removed to assist
viewing in its home in the
Science Museum, South
Kensington. *John Glover*

Below left:
T class electric compartment
stock was introduced in 1927 for
Watford line services. A
standard 6-car formation is seen
at Harrow-on-the-Hill. *LRT*

Right:
Signalling in 1947 was
controlled from small power
frames such as this installation
for the Metropolitan Line at
Baker Street. *LRT*

Below:
Metro-Cammell built a series of
experimental tube cars in
1935-36. Most were streamlined
as in this picture of a two-car
unit. The production series of
1938 stock did not perpetuate
this feature, and the streamlined
cars were later rebuilt to match.
LRT

Left:
Of the same vintage and with a similar rounded profile are the Waterloo & City line replacement stock built by English Electric for the Southern and which entered service in 1940. A train is entering Bank station. *John Glover*

Below:
R stock train approaches Acton Town on a District Line service to Tower Hill. This stock featured the flared 'skirts' which, so it is said, were to deter people from jumping on when the train was leaving and trying to worm their way in through the doors. *John Glover*

Left:
One of the oldest and smallest depots on the system is London Road, Bakerloo Line, seen here with a 1959 stock train leaving. *John Glover*

Below:
The train stop is the basis of Underground safety. The tripcock, seen here in the lowered position, is raised when the signal is at danger. Should a train attempt to pass it, the brakes are applied immediately and the power cut off from the motors. *John Glover*

Bottom:
Train washing is performed by machines on the reception roads of train depots. An R stock train enters Upminster, with the red waist stripe then applied to this stock. *LRT*

Left:
The 1960 Cravens stock was converted to ATO and used on the Woodford-Hainault service. A train is seen at the latter terminus. *John Glover*

Below left:
New stock for the in-town lines of the Metropolitan District and the Circle was delivered from 1970. A C69 train was photographed at Monument. *John Glover*

Below:
Standard stock may still be found in revenue earning service on the remaining Isle of Wight railways operated by British Rail. A seven-car formation descends to Ryde Tunnel in 1980, whose restricted dimensions resulted in the decision to use former tube stock. *John Glover*

Right:
The escalator shafts at Earls Court leading to the Exhibition hall have been restored using the original lighting columns, as could once be seen throughout the system. *John Glover*

Left:
Blake Hall, Essex, closed on
2 November 1981. This country
station is one of the very few to
have closed in postwar years.
John Glover

Below left:
The interiors of the 1983 stock
resemble small scale versions of
the D78 trains. The mixed
transverse and longitudinal
seating may be seen in this view
of a Driving Motor car.
John Glover

Right:
Battery locomotive No L24
heads an engineer's train in the
new step-plate junction tunnel,
installed as part of the
Terminal 4 loop, to link up with
the original over-run tunnels
west of Heathrow Terminals 1, 2,
3. *LRT*

Below:
The Permanent Way Engineer
had taken delivery of a Unimog
vehicle with road and rail
capability. It is used for
autumnal leaf clearing duties on
the outer stretches of the
Metropolitan Line. *John Glover*

Left:
The 1967 stock built for the Victoria Line incorporated ATO from new. Driving Motor Car No 3179 was photographed at Neasden. *John Glover*

Right:
The Tunnel Cleaning Train is formed of former 1938 cars and purpose built trailers. Two filter cars unload dust collected by the nozzle car. *John Glover*

Below right:
A60 stock Driving Motor Car No 5103 stands on the traverser at Acton Works. *John Glover*

Below:
D78 stock deliveries were delayed by the need to incorporate additional ventilation. An unmodified set runs into Cannon Street with a Richmond train. *John Glover*

5
Signalling and Track

Passengers on London's Underground are safer by comparison than on any other form of transport. This is remarkable, considering the extreme density of Underground traffic, where the headway between trains can be as little as 90 seconds. Safe working under these or less exacting conditions is made possible by very efficient signalling, coupled with safety devices that automatically come into play should either the human element or mechanical defect supervene. The most important advance in safety measures was the adoption of automatic signalling, whereby each train alternately protects itself and clears the road behind by completing various electrical circuits in its passage. In earlier Underground days a system of block signalling was in force whereby a train was not permitted to leave a station until the train in front had left the station in advance. This system sufficed when not more than some 800 trains a day worked in and out of Baker Street Metropolitan Station, but now the figure has risen to 1,000 or more, and this increase is reflected to a lesser or greater degree throughout the system. Obviously the advent of the electric train, with greatly increased powers of acceleration and deceleration, required a more flexible signalling system if its advantages were to become fully apparent.

Automatic signalling is no new invention, since it was adopted by the Metropolitan and London Electric Railways in 1905 and 1907 respectively, and earlier still on certain main line railways. The system in use on the Underground has marked advantages over manual signal operation; for one thing it permits a very close headway between trains without the least sacrifice in safety.

The automatic signalling system operates as follows. On passing the starting signal, and in so doing, entering the track circuit section which the signal in part controls, the wheels and axles bridge the running rails and provide an easier path for the signal current than through the signal relay. The relay is thus de-energised, its contacts open, and the signal is restored to red, thereby protecting the train from being overtaken in the rear. As soon as the train has cleared the section, plus an overlap to ensure a margin ahead of a train close on its tail, the short circuit is removed, the signal relay is re-energised, and the normal signal — green — is restored, freeing the rearward circulation. Now if a length of line between two signalboxes is split up into several sections, it follows that two or more trains can enter this length without waiting for one signalman to communicate with the next. Increased line capacity is thus one advantage, and the other is increased safety, for safety devices known as automatic train stops take the control of the train completely out of the driver's hands should he fail to stop at a signal showing red and commanding him to do so.

An arm on the train stop apparatus, placed alongside and worked in conjunction with the stop signal, lies below the running rail level so long as the signal shows clear, but is automatically raised when the signal changes to danger behind a passing train. In this position, the trip arm is pre-set to make contact with a trip cock on the train, should the latter attempt to ignore the signal, and thereupon the cock is opened, releasing compressed air from the train pipe and applying the brakes. The arm of the train stop automatically drops to the non-effective position as soon as the section ahead has been cleared.

With this system there must be a safeguard against possible failure of the train-stop arm to rise when it should, and in such an event, an electric proving circuit holds the preceding signal at danger until the fault in the train stop apparatus has been rectified.

Before leaving this subject it should be mentioned that no driver relishes the prospect of having his train pulled up by the train stop. Such an occurrence normally means that he has negelected to stop at a signal showing danger; and in resetting the trip cock he has incurred delay for which he will have to answer.

On the Underground system, red colour-light signals denote 'Stop' or danger; green denote 'Proceed', and yellow 'Caution Signal ahead at danger'. The colour lights are known as 'aspects' and two-aspect signalling is now standard.

Yellow is used solely to repeat a red aspect in advance which may be out of view of the driver through curvature in tunnel or hidden behind a bridge. On Underground lines the *Fog Repeater* signal has superseded the familiar fog detonator. It is similar to the ordinary repeater and serves the same purpose, but is placed at about the level of the driver's vision and can be seen even in thick fog, or falling snow. Its aspects are emphasised by a white surround with the words 'fog repeater' above them, and the letter 'F' inset in the yellow signal glass. It is switched on only when necessary.

Normally every junction is controlled by a *Semi-Automatic Stop* signal, which bears the code letter or letters of the controlling signalbox, followed by the number of the lever operating the signal. Its normal aspect is red, whereas normal aspect of the standard automatic signal is green. It is known as a 'semi-automatic' because the signal has to be 'cleared' by the deliberate action of a signalman, and reverts to danger automatically after the train has passed, whether or not the controlling lever has been returned to its normal position in the frame. The signal can also be made fully automatic where a signalbox or cabin is not continuously manned. When it is necessary to switch out the box, a 'king lever' movement in the cabin locks certain levers in position for 'through' working, and what was a controlled section becomes automatic.

Another signal is the *Junction Indicator*, with a row of lamps in line pointing in the direction of the set route. Where routes diverge from each side of a through route, there may be a double indicator with directional lights disposed in 'V' formation. In this case, absence of directional lighting indicates that the centre or 'through' route is set.

At the entrance to sidings it is usual to install a *Theatre Type Route Indicator*, wherein small lights behind concentrating lenses make up illuminated numerals on a panel. Any number up to 19 can be automatically reproduced, thereby indicating to drivers the particular siding road they are about to enter. Entry to sidings is controlled by a *Shunt* signal displayng a white disc with a red horizontal bar which rotates to the inclined aspect as indication to 'proceed'. Where the illuminated route indicator is in use, it is usually placed above the shunt disc, with which it acts simultaneously. Shunt signals in modern installations are controlled pneumatically.

The function of the *Platform Starter Repeater* signal is suggested in its name, to indicate to the guard and platform staff the particular aspect displayed at the driver's starting signal, which the guard cannot normally see, especially if the platform is built on a curve. At District and Metropolitan stations the guard used many years ago to give the right-away to the driver by bridging a pair of suspended electrified wires with the brass sleeve of his flag handle, which caused a letter 'S' to appear in lights under the starting signal, while a bell 'reminder' was set ringing. With the extension of guard's panel control, however, this system was removed.

Speed restrictions are usually made known to drivers by means of track signs showing the speed limit in large numerals with a sign bearing a large 'T', to indicate termination of the length affected, but speed restrictions can also be imposed through the medium of the normal signalling.

There is a rather interesting example on the southbound run from High Barnet. The gradient falls sharply into the tunnel at East Finchley and continues to fall at 1 in 50 all the way to Archway station. On the stretch between Highgate and Archway it is necessary to keep the speed within certain limits because of the sharp curve to be negotiated just before entering Archway station.

Two timing sections were therefore arranged on this portion of line to limit the speed of trains. The first section controls a signal about 200yd beyond it, which will not clear if the train exceeds 40mph over the timing length. The second section controls a signal about 100yd beyond it and 250yd from the curve, which will not clear to any train exceeding 30mph over the second length. In this way, speed has been reduced so that the curve cannot be taken too fast, even though the speeding driver should attempt to do so, because in the event the automatic train stop would come into action.

A later development was the instant speed detector signal, which was designed to ease the accumulative checkback of trains working to a close schedule over lines where stations are close together, and where it is likely that trains may be held in such stations for more than 30 seconds. Its purpose is primarily to enable the home signal to be cleared earlier, *providing essentially that the train approaching it is travelling at the required reduced speed.* The newer device does not require a fixed length of track to enable the average speed to be determined, but instead assesses the speed at a given point, in this wise:

A 12ft length of stainless steel rail is fitted to the side of the track, where the shoes will contact it, in advance of the related signal. To the underside of the rail are fitted 12 permanent magnets and coils 9in apart. The train's positive shoes pass over the rail, and in so doing cause a small alternating current to be generated in the coil. The frequency of the current varies exactly in proportion to the train's speed over the magnets, and hence is a measure of that speed. A relay connected responds only to alternating current below a given frequency, and only when the relay operates does the signal ahead clear. Measurements correct to half a mile an hour are said to have been achieved with this apparatus, whose accuracy is contributed to by the fact that the detector makes constant checks as each of the train shoes passes over the inductors. It will be seen that the necessity for the driver to judge his speed correctly at this critical spot is thereby obviated.

The foregoing is an outline of signalling as seen and experienced from the cab: a description of signal regulation, and the work of signalmen generally, would normally complete the picture. But the whole concept of Underground signalling is changing with the need to regulate one of the most densely-worked rail networks in the world — and to keep just ahead in development in order to do so. In the past it was necessary for signalmen and their equipment to be located at or near the junction or intersection of tracks, in order to control their sections, and in consequence there were many signalboxes and many signalmen. Today there are fewer, and tomorrow there may be none; that is, as we normally visualise them. Electronic operation is taking over, and robot-like apparatus can work without the aid of human hands. Nevertheless the writer feels he cannot just portray the modern system without a brief look backwards, to illustrate the progress already made in signal engineering.

Some years ago he was invited to inspect the then modernised signalbox at Aldgate, controlling as it still does a busy junction complex at the eastern end of the Circle Line. Actually there are three junctions at the triangle of tracks formed by parts of the Inner Circle, the Metropolitan and the District Lines. In the cabin or box a long power frame of miniature levers is worked by signalmen who handle at peak periods (or did at that time) as many as 120 trains per hour. Above the frame an illuminated diagram gives a picture of the various tracks and the position of trains moving over them. Trains are 'advised' to the cabin on a train describer panel, and are described on a transmitter as they are dispatched away from the controlled area. Signalmen receive trains by 'pulling off' a signal after setting the road where necessary. These signals are of the semi-automatic type previously referred to and are restored to danger by the passage of trains past them. The signal cannot clear again until the signalman has restored his lever to normal and 'restroked', or reversed it. The levers have both electrical and mechanical locking as safeguards against irregular movement.

'Back-locking' relay apparatus prevents a signalman from inadvertently replacing a lever and resetting a road when once a train has accepted the signal, and mechanical locks block the movement of any lever, other than the one pulled, that could set up a conflicting movement. Below the cabin is a room housing 266 relays in a glass-fronted covers to protect them from dust and damp. More than 50 miles of wire was needed to complete the circuiting in this room when the equipment was installed.

Such, in brief, is a manned signal cabin; but remote control of cabins has been in operation for some years. A cabin may be switched out and its functions controlled from a distant cabin; or it may be designed for remote control as normal, and for manual operation at short notice if necessary. In these instances the levers may be manipulated by electro-pneumatic apparatus from the distant cabin, where such manipulation of a remotely controlled lever would also operate the requisite points and so 'set-up' a route.

It was obvious that further automation would eventually be applied to underground signalling, consistent with safety: and it was taking the form in this instance of the Programme Machine.

Remote control, push-button, route-setting signalling was a development of automatic signalling, whereby each train protects itself through track circuiting; programme signalling is best described by reference to machines that were widely installed over the system. If we say that remote control signalling carries the decision of a signalman over a distance, then transforms it into route-setting, and advises the driver through visible signals, then programme signalling does this automatically and reliably without the signalman. We have seen as an example that in one peak hour 1,200 trains pass through a complex of junctions (at Aldgate). On many junctions, reversing points, sidings and the like on the Underground system, numbers of programme machines signalled vast numbers of trains daily, with consequent increased efficiency in daily running and a big saving in man power.

Machines installed on the Underground system at the moment of writing automatically set up individual routes for trains, sometimes over long distances, but excepting those tracks within depots and similar places. (This applies to route-setting through junctions, etc. Over plain track, of course, signalling is automatic, actuated by the train itself through track circuiting.)

In essence it is a memory machine equipped with details which include trains' destinations, their numbers, and their times recorded on a plastic roll 8in wide and 8ft long. Actually the holes punched in the roll are a code of this information. Probe contacts in an assembly pressed against the roll by compressed air read particulars of the first train to approach the junction and signal it accordingly. As the train proceeds it energises a relay and puts apparatus in motion to lift the contacts clear of the coded roll whilst it moves one step, corresponding to one train movement. The movement completed, the motor rotating the roll stops and the contact assembly is once again pressed against the roll to probe, read and signal the description of the next train.

The programme machine is arranged to check the train description, as received on the train describer, with the description, as shown on the timetable, and, provided they agree, the train is automatically signalled through. The sequence is in effect thus: trains despatched form, say, Edgware are described by the signalman there. Train describer apparatus at Camden Town receives descriptions and stores them. The programme machine checks and releases, in timetable sequence, information that is fed electrically to interlocking machines, which automatically operate the signals and points mechanisms. The plastic roll is automatically rewound after completion of the day's timetable so that it is ready to begin again next morning, but in the later type of machine the rewinding is done on Monday, Tuesday, Wednesday and Thursday nights. At the end of the Friday timetable the machine carries straight on, working through the Saturday and then the Sunday timetable, which are coded on a continuation of the week day roll. At the end of the Sunday timetable the whole roll is rewound ready for Monday morning. This obviates the manual replacement of weekday by separate Saturday and Sunday rolls.

The interlocking machine referred to comprises a safety signalling system. The machine has shafts, one to each set of points or crossover, or each signal. These shafts, operated by compressed air, are mechanically interlocked and control the safety points and signal circuits so as to prevent any dangerous situation arising from failure of the controlling system.

It was a fairly obvious trend that as all the machines between them controlled many small and separate areas, their activities should be under the supervision of centrally situated control centres, where the areas can be watched from a distance, as it were, and adjustments made in the running of trains whenever these are necessary. The control centres, or signal regulating rooms, have been established at strategic points. One at Euston (Cobourg Street) now supervises and regulates the Northern and Victoria Lines. One at Earls Court now supervises the Piccadilly and District Lines. Also, at Baker Street, two control and regulating rooms supervise the Bakerloo and Central Lines, and the Metropolitan and Jubilee Lines respectively. At these Centres, illuminated diagrams provide programme information, ie next approaching train numbers and destinations, and the position of every train in the area under programme control

We qualified the use of programme machines by saying they *were* widely installed over the system. But today, as a step towards eventual automation on all the Underground system, computers are being increasingly brought in to facilitate the system's signalling operations.

For some time now such computers (working in duplicate) have exercised local control over train movement at Heathrow Central in the same way as the programme machine they replaced. And they are also being provided in the central control rooms to facilitate centralised control functions.

It is beyond the scope of this book to attempt any detailed description of the computer except to say that it takes over the function of the programme machine up to that of the interlocking machine, occupies less space, and is able to carry out instructions, but not yet to formulate them. So that for the task of automatically controlling the programme machines, for instance, operating the Northern and Victoria Lines, the computer would require first to be fed with all the detail of these lines' running.

This it is supplied with in the form of the timetable from London Transport's Data Processing Department; and in its completed form — that is, after checks and corrections for possible conflict situations — this data is converted to punched paper tape, and magnetic tape in proportion.

But already the operation of programme machine and computer signalling is virtually automatic in so far as it is able, for instance, to adjust services that have got out of timetable sequence. Even so, the system still needs a Regulator's constant attention, whose duties tend to become exacting if, for example, he has to normalise a situation that has become disorganised (say through delays and cancellations) and also to inform colleagues elsewhere of what steps he has taken. Some of this work can be assigned to the computer.

This computer is able to perform a variety of functions, including storage and release in the form of instructions of data it has received, plus the many modifications that may subsequently have been added; to provide visual displays in colour of information for the guidance of Controllers, Regulators, and information to those requiring it at stations and car depots; to keep periodic check on train services, and to adjust them to best acceptable levels for the public in the event of cancellations, delays and the like.

The safety signalling system mentioned earlier is of course incorporated in all signalling installations, whether they be machine, computer or manually operated.

Finally, modern two-way radio is being progressively introduced on trains, both surface and Tube stock. It is mentioned in this signalling section of the book since signal engineers are concerned with the design and planning. The last line to be equipped will be the Victoria Line, which already has carrier wave communication with Control, but this is subject to a degree of interference that modern two-way radio escapes. Briefly, the latter allows continuous communication with trains, moving or stationary — and is part of a long-term signal and communication plan which envisages positive identification of any train and its precise position on a line.

The foregoing is no more than a basic description of signalling on London's Underground: but the writer shares with London Transport the hope that as a result of new methods and procedures that have been, or may be applied, the travelling public will benefit from a progressive improvement of the train services, and concurrently will be better informed about them through public address systems.

Close to the huge Exhibition building at Earls Court is the Lillie Bridge Permanent Way Depot, where track units for London's Underground are manufactured. Raw material in the shape of 60ft lengths of rail is delivered here from the rolling mills, coming via trunk railways and the West London Extension Railway, which flanks the depot.

The site was originally acquired in the 1870s by the District Railway Company for its engine sheds and rolling stock. Years later, after the District had moved its works elsewhere, the Great Northern, Piccadilly & Brompton Railway in 1906 used the site for car sheds, reaching it from where its tube surfaced near Barons Court station, via a short stretch of District line. The Piccadilly vacated the site for its then new car depot at Northfields in 1932, by which time the Lillie Bridge Depot had developed into the Underground's Permanent Way Depot, with all the equipment necessary for maintaining the permanent way.

In 1932 it had only just been reconstructed and a new workshop and stores building erected for the overhaul, among other things, of signal equipment. Tracks, road, sleeper, rail and chair stacks were all rearranged as part of a very long modernisation scheme; but as the Underground's requirements grew, so the depot's limitations became apparent.

Space was a major consideration, and although up to 1969 improvements were still being made, one of the depot's principal functions, the welding of 60ft lengths of running rail into one continuous 300ft long rail, by means of a flash-butt welding machine, was taken from Lillie Bridge and begun at the West Ruislip Car Depot in that year. (Rail welding will be described in the section devoted to Car Depots.) The car shed previously used for welding was converted into two separate working areas, one for the maintenance of battery cars and the other for use as a welding and crossing making shop where an overhead crane of 54cwt capacity was installed.

Trains carrying assembled tracks, etc leave the depot and enter the Underground system via West Kensington on the District Line. The depot yard, which has several tracks or roads, is straddled by a traverser crane, well named the 'Goliath', with a 100ft span and a 1,000ft run, which picks up and deposits seven-ton loads from any point to any other. A bar magnet capable of lifting 60ft rails can substitute the normal hook and chain lifting gear.

The manufacturing scope of the depot is surprising. At the heavy end of the scale are points and crossings and at the other end are coach screws and insulator clips. Construction, however, by no means comprises all the work of the depot, for it is responsible, among other things, for the storage of materials used for day-to-day track maintenance, including conductor rail, and the renewal thereof, the upkeep of embankments, fencing, sewers, surface drains, tunnel drainage, and, very important this, the work of construction. Here also is the main railway stores depot and the signal department overhaul and test shop. In 1983 Ashfield House situated east of West Kensington station was erected. This new eight-storey building centralised the offices of the Civil Engineering Departments under one roof.

To give some idea of the varied nature of the Depot's workshop staffs it can be said that the following trades are represented: fitters, tinsmiths, electricians, blacksmiths, welders, carpenters, machinists, turners, and points and crossing fitters.

In the *Machine Shop* situated in the main block the variety of work includes all planing work for the production of points and crossings. An unusual feature of this shop is that it includes blacksmiths' forges which manufacture and repair tools, brackets, signal equipment and fishplates of all types. The fitting section is also here where work includes manufacture of precision gauges, jigs, special track equipment such as oil boxes and tool cabin equipment plus maintenance of hydraulic and mechanical jacks. An overhead runway carrying a 2-ton crane conveys light and heavy material from an outside arrival bay to individual machines via points on the main runway, controlled from a central panel. Load raising and lowering is operated from the crane.

Welding and Crossing Makers' Shop. This work is vital for the safety of the travelling public. Design of points and crossings is not static. It must ensure that the appropriate type of equipment is provided at each particular site. Manufactured components including splice rails are drilled, bent and finished off in accordance with machining details and later assembled in position on lay-out ground. The area vacated by transference to West Ruislip of long rail manufacture now accommodates electric battery trains. Cutting and drilling running rail other than long welded rail, manufacture of conductor rail and rail-built buffer stops, plus gas, electric arc and oxy-acetylene welding are just part of this shop's activities.

Also manufactured here are the oil baths used for high rail and check rail lubrication. Their purpose is to lubricate the wheel flanges of passing trains to minimise the grinding action of wheel against rail. The high rail referred to is the outer running rail laid on curves. It is laid higher than the inner rail to counteract the outward throw of centrifugal force on the moving train, thereby canting the coaches, and it is on acute curves, where grinding action is most severe that the oil baths are placed.

Bridge timber renewal, current-rail safety boards and wooden walkways are part of the work carried out in the carpenter's shop whilst the plant maintenance shop looks after the great variety of portable powered and fixed tools etc. Inspections of incoming material are made by the Chief Civil Engineer's Inspection Staff. But obviously the vast London Transport network generates an equally vast amount of benchwork and the like unable, for space reasons to be mentioned here.

The standard running rail on the London Transport system is of 95lb/yd bull-headed section, secured by oak or steel keys to chairs, which are coach-screwed to the sleepers. Conductor rail is of 130lb/yd rectangular section in tube tunnels, and 150lb flat bottom section elsewhere. Flat-bottomed rail and concrete sleepers are gradually being introduced in open sections. The new Heathrow extension uses F.B. rail laid on specially designed concrete sleepers.

In tunnel sections the sleepers, spaced 3ft 4in apart, are of Australian Jarrah wood (which is almost indestructible), and in the open they are of creosoted fir or similar wood, spaced 2ft 7in apart, except at rail joints, where the spacing is reduced. To lessen the work of track maintenance, sleeper ends in tunnels are rigidly supported in concrete, and the tunnel invert below is filled up to sleeper level with ballast, which has the effect of deadening the clangour of trains passing through the iron tunnel lining.

And here is an interesting point concerning rails in bay roads, where the track is not in continuous use and quickly rusts, impeding the flow of low-tension current for the track circuits. The bright idea of depositing stainless steel on the rail head was successfully put into practice, and now one may see little-used bay roads with a continuous narrow, wavy band of stainless steel deposit on the top of the running rail.

With regard to the operation of points, it is perhaps already known that this is normally accomplished by means of compressed air. Movements actuated by signalling apparatus complete a number of electrical circuits, one of which opens a valve to admit compressed air to the cylinder of an air engine placed alongside the points, and the ensuing thrust of the piston puts the points over.

Despite its space limitations, Lillie Bridge Depot is still, and is likely to remain, the permanent way maintenance centre for the Underground system. It cannot be expanded due to its being surrounded by railways and built-up property, but the site has a unique advantage in so far as it lies at the geographical centre of the system. Through rail connections, it is linked to the trunk railways, mainly for supply; and for distribution of its products, together with actual works trains, it can be reached from all parts of the Underground by the shortest route — a vital consideration when working time consists of those few night hours when passenger trains are not running.

Permanent-way men on the Underground carry out a large part of their work whilst others sleep. This is particularly true where work has to be done in tunnels, in which case a job usually has to be started and finished during the five hours per night when the line is shut down and current switched off.

The system is divided into open, tube and sub-surface sections known as PW Divisions, responsible for the maintenance and renewal of the permanent way by inspection and track staff (excepting that connected with signals). Trackmen work under a leading ganger and ganger. The inspector, responsible for his section, decides what work if any requires to be done.

Permanent-way work necessarily comes least before the public eye, but together with signal maintenance it is the most important on a railway system. Your safety and mine depends on a true 4ft 8½in gauge, properly cambered, graded, ballasted, and generally maintained; and it is the permanent-way man who sees to all these things.

Right:
Most of the Underground's power supply comes from Lots Road; this view shows the control room. *LRT*

Below:
One person operation without automatic train control is now in operation on most of the surface lines network. At Fulham Broadway in June 1985, a mirror combined with a cctv monitor is being installed. *John Glover*

6
Power Stations and Passenger Stations

Some years ago the writer visited London Transport's Lots Road Generating Station and described it in previous issues of this book. He wrote then that thin plumes of smoke drifting from its tall chimneys gave little indication of the tremendous potential energy being generated within. He said that three such stations, at Neasden, Greenwich and Chelsea (Lots Road) provided much of the power to energise the London Underground system, and some power was bought from the Central Electricity Generating Board. Energy at Lots Road was taken in in the form of small-grained 'pea' coal, and of every 100 tons of coal burned, nearly 80% was lost in converting it into electricity, leaving 20% as pure 'juice'.

On a later visit he expected, and found much alteration. Plumes of smoke no longer drift from the Lots Road station's tall chimneys, as the vast building was literally disembowelled of its boilers, alternators and other equipment to make way for the new steam-raising plant and new generators. With their installation, and change of energising fuel from coal to oil or natural gas, the station's power output has been increased to cope with (among other things) the Victoria and Jubilee Lines. The modernisation made possible and roughly coincided with the closure in 1968 of the Neasden power station.

At Lots Road the old warm, gently roaring power house with its glowing, slowly moving chain grates; its glistening rows of humming generators; and its parquet-floored control room, all knobbly with polished dials and instruments, is a nostalgic memory.

In its place is pastel-coloured, hygienic, computer-assisted efficiency. Visibly there is less evidence of motion than before — everything is seemingly encased and smoothed-out. The two new and bigger turbo-alternators installed show only glimpses of shafts, spinning at 3,000rpm as against the older generators' 2,000rpm.

The station is situated on the north bank of the Thames, with the old coal bunkers, now housing its oil storage tanks, on one side of Chelsea Creek and the power house on the other. The power station, originally built to serve the Metropolitan, District, the Baker Street & Waterloo, the Piccadilly, and the Charing Cross, Euston & Hampstead Railways, was opened in 1905. It was then claimed to be one of the biggest generating stations in the world and today still dominates the riverside. Jutting out unseen into the river bed are two huge water-intake pipes, of 9ft and 7ft 9in respectively, supplying the station with its largest commodity, cooling water, of which a staggering total of some seven million gallons per hour is needed when the station is on full load. The water passes first through screens to remove debris, and is then used to cool the condensers, where it acquires heat, finally re-entering the river via Chelsea Creek, 11°F warmer than before (of piscatorial rather than technical interest is the fact that today, fish are periodically netted and tossed back into the river after being sucked willy-nilly into the inlet basin).

So much for the cooling water, but that used in the boilers for steam-raising is a different proposition. It must not be such as to leave scale deposit in tubes or on turbine blades. Therefore it is freed of dissolved salts by several chemical processes after being pumped from a 300ft deep well, which Lots Road fortunately possesses and which has never yet run dry.

It is at the steam producing stage that changes from old to new are most marked. There were once 32 hopper-fed coal-burning boilers to provide steam for nine turbo-alternators. Now there are but six vertical oil-fired boilers to serve six turbo-alternators, and it follows that the new boilers are larger, both in size and steam-producing capability. A striking feature is that they are actually suspended from beams above one's head, on a structure 100ft high. This allows for flexibility, necessary as the boiler structure itself expands several inches when fully heated. Another notable feature is that the furnace walls actually form the boiler. The walls are in fact membrane structures of boiler tubes, each tube welded together throughout its length to its neighbour.

Through a small aperture when a door is opened one can see (standing at a respectful distance) the furnace burners fanning out a great plume of flame, the product of ignited gas and hot air under forced draught. It should be emphasised here that although the policy is to use natural gas as the normal fuel in so far as it is cheaper than heavy fuel oil, the furnace is constructed to burn either. (The ability to use either fuel also gives greater flexibility, as well as ensuring continued electricity supply for most of London's Underground should the supply of one or the other be interrupted.)

Steam is hot when it leaves the boiler tubes to be collected into a thick steel tank above, whence it is again led through tubes within the furnace. This superheats the steam, raising its temperature to 935°F before it passes initially through high-pressure turbine blading, then at lower temperature through low-pressure blading, and finally as condensate back into the boilers.

The turbines coupled with their generators are massive single pieces of machinery, weighing in total 254 tons and bedded rock-like to steel and concrete. The turbine-driven generator produces electric current; in brief, by the rotor (an electromagnet) revolving within the outer 'stator', producing alternating current at 22,000V. Some of this is transformed to lower voltages for power house motors, etc.

In the new instrument room, placed in plan between boiler and generating areas, operators are informed by dials and indicators of the state of both boiler and generator performance, but the final control of both generation and distribution of the electric power is in a separate building, in the large, quiet control room. The senior operator on duty at a central desk can see the long desk fitted with switches and dials from which the station's entire output is controlled, and behind it the 'mimic' diagram providing an up-to-the-minute record of the state of the power distribution system. The actual regulation and switching operates on remote relay-control principles, which in essence means that dangerous high-voltage electricity is distantly and indirectly controlled by low-voltage equipment. At all times, in any case, this concentration of high-tension current is well insulated and virtually 'locked up', so that any approach to its conductors or switching, for adjustment, is made a deliberate and purposeful job, like opening a safe.

The foregoing is of course only a generally descriptive outline of Lots Road Generating Station. The following details may help to fill it in somewhat. The new boiler drums are 25ft 9¼in long and 5ft in internal diameter. The furnace height is 67ft. Turbo-generators are 58ft 8in in overall length, and their revolving parts weigh in total 41¾ tons. Maximum tip speed (that at the tips of the turbine low-pressure blades) is 715mph, as against 511mph in the older turbo-generators. Voltage generated is 22,000 at 50 cycles per second (now called 50 'Hertz') as against 11,000 at 331/3 Hz previously. The total capacity of the old plant was 168,750 kilowatts, which was increased to 180,000kW by the modernisation.

Greenwich Power Station has also been vastly altered. Smaller than Lots Road, with an installed capacity of 112,000kW, its steam plant was replaced over a period until 1972 by gas turbine alternators. Like the bigger station, it also uses gas or oil as fuel. The station is remotely controlled from Lots Road and operated in parallel with Lots Road through 22kV nitrogen-filled cables.

(A report in 1983 mentioned the possibility of London Transport eventually taking all its power from the national grid, a cheaper source of electricity. Lots Road would be closed and the Greenwich station would cease to be a feeding point — but it would take about 15 years to effect this proposed change, when Lots Road would have reached the end of its useful life.)

From Lots Road the power lines run to Stockwell, Cobourg Street and Cromwell Curve switch houses, where transformers reduce the voltage to 11,000V, for distribution to substations.

The function of substation equipment on the underground is to receive high tension current, step it down to traction voltage (ie, the pressure required by the trains, in this case 600V), and rectify the supply from alternating current as generated to direct current as delivered to the traction motors. The current then flows through track feeders to the conductor rail, each length of conductor rail being, of course, bonded or welded to its neighbour.

Over the whole of the system London Transport has at present 109 substations serving its railways, and there are also substations which belong to British Railways but serve London Transport trains which run over BR metals. Of late years substations have been built to, or adapted to, operate automatically and unmanned. Generally these substations transformed high-voltage current to lower voltages and rectified it from ac to dc by means of rotary transformers. But ultimately the latter were replaced by mercury arc equipment, and in some cases silicon rectifying equipment. This 'static' equipment has the advantage of occupying less space than rotary converters and also lends itself more to automatic operation. Overall, there are safety features which are basically retained, the principle being that the flow of high tension current or lower tension traction current can be cut, or is automatically cut, by the action of circuit breakers — an instance being when current had to be cut off from a section of tunnel track by a motorman, through breakdown or other emergency. By pinching together and so short-circuiting two bare wires laid along the tunnel wall, he actuates a substation relay, which in turn trips the track breakers.

The whole subject of power generation and distribution is too vast to be dealt with at length in this book, but there can be occasions when the reader, if he so wished, could think of it more personally. It could be during those week-night peak hours, when trains crossing London increasingly fill with people making their way home. The train doors close, the motorman gets his signal and notches up, away from the station platform into the tunnel. The motors take on the work of accelerating a heavily-laden train, and call for more power to do so.

Back in the generating station, operators have already braced themselves, so to speak, for the nightly peak. More power is called for and more is switched in until the power curves up to satisfy full load (but never to the limit, there are always reserves at hand). Men in the power stations are always aware of their responsibilities to the travelling public, but each working week-night from about 5 o'clock to 6.30 their responsibilities are surely intensified, all the time the trains are coping with hundreds of thousands of dependent homegoers. Gradually the laden trains empty London, the trains themselves empty, some are stabled and the load curves down. The station relaxes — until next morning, when the cycle starts all over again.

The writer, a good deal older since first he became one of London's commuters, tends like others to forget the prime sources of motive power that carry him about London's underground; until he is permitted to revisit its biggest source at Lots Road, where he renews his respect for that power, and for the men who handle it.

Passenger stations
There are at present 272 passenger stations served by London Transport trains including Heathrow Terminal 4, but this total never remains constant

for more than a few years. Their variety is almost infinite, ranging from structures of the trussed roof type as at Earls Court, reminiscent of steam days and the past in general, to the ultra-modern type built for this age and the next, where airiness and simplicity in design are in keeping with these times of electric traction. The busiest stations in terms of passenger use, are Victoria (48million passengers a year), Oxford Circus (39million), King's Cross (32million) and Liverpool Street (30million). These numbers exclude those interchanging between lines.

As already mentioned, several Inner London stations have been reconstructed, or built anew on a different site. This work entails the most complicated of all underground engineering when such things as subways, sewers, mains and even tunnels may have to be stopped, diverted or otherwise accommodated. Engineers have not only these things to consider, but they must always make provision in their plans for the daily traffic, which never ceases. One of the biggest jobs of reconstruction, at King's Cross, merits a description as it involved major work over several years ending 1941, and further major works in the 1960s to accommodate the Victoria Line.

King's Cross Station (London Transport) is a labyrinth of passages, shafts and tunnels where five lines meet — the Metropolitan and Circle, Piccadilly, Northern and Victoria Lines. At one time the Metropolitan station was situated several hundred yards east of King's Cross, roughly beneath the junction of Caledonian and Pentonville Roads. To reach it from King's Cross main line station meant a long walk, but after it was closed and the present one opened there was, and is, only a short walk through a subway from the present ticket hall under the main line forecourt.

This serves the Piccadilly, Northern and Victoria tubes and, through subways, St Pancras and King's Cross main line stations. Escalator shafts lead downwards first to the Victoria Line at 50ft, the Piccadilly at 56ft, and further down still to the Northern Line.

As usual, most of the work on this project had to be done whilst the stations were coping with heavy passenger traffic, and whilst Euston Road was carrying its normal great volume of surface traffic.

It will add interest to an account of this undertaking if we imagine the layout of roads and railways at this point. Euston Road runs roughly east and west past the frontages of St Pancras and King's Cross stations; 35ft below lies the Metropolitan Line, which follows the course of the roadway. A tunnel curves out from beneath St Pancras, carrying the tracks of the widened lines which meet the Metropolitan and run alongside it to Moorgate. The tunnels connecting the widened lines with the Great Northern at King's Cross were abandoned in 1976. West of the point where the tunnels converge, and running parallel with the Metropolitan, was a short length of abandoned tunnel, built in 1868 towards Euston Square, but never completed. This is the picture at sub-surface level.

About 50ft below the Metropolitan junction tunnels are those of the

Piccadilly, set wide apart and crossing obliquely. Sandwiched between the Midland (St Pancras) Curve and Circle tunnels and the Piccadilly tunnels are those of the Victoria Line, with the Northern Line at the lowest of all three levels.

Connecting the northbound tracks of the Piccadilly and Northern Lines is a single line tunnel, which Northern Line rolling stock destined for Acton Works uses to reach the Piccadilly Line, and thence travels to Acton.

To provide for the new Metropolitan station, the eastbound Metropolitan track was diverted into the abandoned tunnel just mentioned, and a new tunnel was constructed on the south side of the main Metropolitan tunnel. This enabled the redundant portion of the main tunnel to be used partly as an entrance and a ticket hall, and partly to provide for a reversing bay, although this was never electrified and was partly filled in. Additional space was thus secured for passenger circulation because the main tunnel was generously proportioned to accommodate a double track of the old GW seven-foot gauge; the reversing bay has also been removed and its site used as a passenger concourse.*

There were difficulties both above and below ground. The dense traffic along Euston Road was kept moving over a large hole (exposing the Metropolitan and St Pancras tunnel lines below) only by bridging it with tremendous girders. Then the 70-year old abandoned tunnel, wet and layered with accumulated dirt, had to be cleaned and waterproofed to fit it for its new use.

So ended the first King's Cross reconstruction. The second project undertaken 20 years later included the positioning and building of the new Victoria Line underground station, which meant excavating two horizontal tunnels, one 12ft and one 15ft diameter, both of them for draught relief and each about 75ft long, connecting the Piccadilly and Victoria Lines' stations to a new vertical air shaft. Then there were the actual Victoria Line station tunnels, 460ft long, to be excavated, and an inclined escalator shaft to link them to the ticket hall above. At this latter level the famous Fleet River sewer meandered through the works area. It had to be diverted and re-contained in a new concrete ring and box construction, which at one point nearly obtrudes into the new ticket hall. One can visualise all this new tunnel construction as being more or less threaded through existing tunnels and shafts, and undertaken in deep earth with no way of pinpointing objectives by sight as one does above ground.

Even then, further reconstruction was to take place in the 1980s when King's Cross Midland Station in Pentonville Road was rebuilt in connection

---

*Incidentally, this is perhaps as good a place as any to observe the massive proportion of the old eliptical tunnel.

with the Midland Suburban Electrification and connected by direct subways to both the Piccadilly and Victoria Lines.

A feature of below-ground tube stations is the track-pit, or trough. Track pits have been the means of saving the lives of many passengers who have fallen on to the track, and another safeguard has been introduced to lessen the risk of passengers missing their footing between the platform and the train.

Where platforms are built on a sharp curve (on the northbound Northern Line at Embankment, for instance), there is a pronounced gap at the centre of each coach which necessarily cuts a deep chord in relation to the curve of a platform. Illuminated signs 'Mind the Gap' carry their warning in addition to an automatic warning over a loudspeaker.

Whilst at one time it was the policy to build stations all more or less alike, today there is a greater variety of station architecture on the London Transport railway system than anywhere else in the world. This results partly from a bold and imaginative policy and partly from circumstances obtaining at the site.

The surface buildings for the Cockfosters extension set a new trend in design, as did others built at roughly the same time. They were rectangular, circular or semicircular, in some cases with a tower concealing a ventilation shaft.

East Finchley on the Northern Line is another striking example of railway architecture. The old station dealt only with steam-hauled traffic and was almost rural in appearance, but the station opened in 1939 is just the opposite, conveying those impressions of streamlined speed associated with fast electric trains. Surmounting one of the walls, the figure of a bowman aiming in the direction of London heightens the impression of swift transit; and it must be admitted that short of a fast car with a pretty clear road, there is no speedier way of reaching Town.

Wanstead station on the north-eastern extension of the Central Line is interesting mainly because of its past, when during the last war it was not much more than a windowless box used in connection with the munition works below.

But it is at Gants Hill that something unique among tube stations can be seen. A roomy station was needed at this point, where several heavy traffic routes converge on Eastern Avenue, the busy trunk road linking London with Southend, and it was decided to improve on the usual design by driving a third large-diameter passenger tunnel between the two station tunnels.

Actually, several interpenetrating tunnels were driven, and all but the outside linings were removed, leaving space for a large concourse, or wide expanse of platform between the running tunnels. The upper half of the centre tunnel lining forms a high, arched roof for the concourse, and is supported by two rows of pillars, massive enough to support the great weight of earth above. The platforms, 485ft in length, are partly carried in standard diameter station tunnels.

Escalators lead to the ticket hall built below a traffic roundabout, and subways radiate to stairs leading to the pavement. In fact, one could rightly term Gants Hill a suburban Piccadilly Circus.

In 1959 another virtually new station at Notting Hill Gate was brought into use. Like all such jobs entailing conversion without closure of busy stations on the Underground, the task was both intricate and massive, and has taken years from its inception to the final completion. Previously there were two stations at Notting Hill, one on each side of Notting Hill Gate, a very busy highway. They served the Circle and Central Lines respectively, and some 2,000,000 passengers who every year wished to change from one line to the other had to cross the busy road on the surface. Today a modern sub-surface station links the two lines by a joint ticket hall, and provides direct interchange facilities by a subway at a lower level. When one realises that the Central eastbound platform is 100ft below surface, the westbound partly above and to one side of it, and the Circle Line some distance away and about 27ft below ground, the complexity of the work can perhaps be visualised.

An Underground reconstruction job within the City of London at Blackfriars Station (one of the oldest on the system) may well interest the historian. Passengers there had once to use a narrow cat-walk to reach the end cars, and in order to lengthen its platforms by 74ft, the running tunnel had to be demolished and replaced by a wider covered way for the platforms.

In 1860, when the station site was excavated, as much as 24ft of made-up ground, ruined buildings and debris going back perhaps two thousand years had to be cut through. The famous Fleet sewer, once a navigable waterway emptying into the River Thames, had to be diverted to run under the tracks, and part of the recent work involved fresh bridging of the sewer. The difficulties of the whole reconstruction job are apparent when it is realised that the water below and the heavy traffic along the roadway above both had to be kept on the move.

Many busy but ageing stations at or near central London have been given a 'face-lift'. At the same time, murals have been applied to walls to depict street scenes above ground. For instance, the mosaics at Tottenham Court Road are of musical instruments, and at Baker Street Station (Circle Line), tiled shafts, once built as vents to clear locomotive steam and smoke and to admit daylight, when the station was built in 1863, now have sodium lights to re-create the original daylight effect.

With the growth of passenger traffic on the Underground, the need arose at many stations for something more effective than a lift to connect the deep platforms with the surface. The ideal aimed at was a conveyance that could deal economically with a steady trickle of passengers, and yet could absorb a surge at peak hours without becoming overloaded or causing congestion. The answer was the escalator, or moving stairs, and it met the situation so adequately that it has been installed wherever possible, not only at deep-level stations, but also at busy points where the rise is sometimes as small as 20ft.

The first escalator for public use on the Underground was installed at Earls Court in 1911. The longest, at Leicester Square Station, at 161.5ft (49.6m) has a vertical rise of 80.75ft (24.6m), whilst the shortest, at Chancery Lane station, 30ft (9.1m), has a vertical rise of only 15ft (4.6m). Originally, passengers had to side-step off escalators, but now they are combed off in a simple, forward movement.

A device to enable long escalators to be run at half their normal speed when unloaded, is installed at some less busy stations. It employs a light sensitive cell whose beam, interrupted or otherwise, governs the motor's speed through relays. Normal service speeds vary according to their location from 95 to 145ft/min.

Escalator tunnels or shafts vary in diameter from 18ft to about 25ft, and may contain one, two, or three escalators. An exception is at Holborn Station, where there are four in a 30ft tunnel. Access to the underside of an escalator is provided in the tunnel invert.

At some stations already fitted with lifts, where the expense of installing escalators would not be justified, an economical improvement in the handling of traffic can be secured by installing high-speed lifts, fully automatic in working. They feature a loudspeaker attachment that automatically warns passengers to stand clear of the closing doors.

Two express lifts at Hampstead, London's deepest tube station, reach a speed of 800ft/min, some 200ft/min faster than express lifts ordinarily travel, as at Goodge Street Station. (Incidentally, passengers on this Hampstead line reach the lowest point on the system, some 300yd north of the station, where they are 250ft below the crest of Hampstead Heath.)

A problem as old as underground railways is that of ventilating the tunnels adequately with economy, and without causing discomfort to passengers or creating nuisance to residents near the ventilating shafts. It was an insoluble problem in steam days, but there were so many other inconveniences associated with horse-drawn surface travel that an intake of sulphurous smoke was considered a fair deal by all, except the large minority who found underground travel actively nauseating. Of course, the problem partly solved itself when steam haulage went, but, even so, to overcome the remaining difficulties has taken years of experiment and research. At one time on the Metropolitan and District simple 'blow holes' covered with a grating provided some relief, and years later the Central London tube installed 'ozonisers' or 'air purifiers', the ducts of which can still be seen here and there at stations. The ozonisers certainly sucked air into the stations, but apparently they ozonified it so highly that its seaside tang clung about the person for some time, and finally condemned the experiment.

Modern practice is to exhaust spent and heated air from the tunnels by means of powerful fans discharging into specal ducts, and to admit fresh air through the natural channels of station entrances, staircase shafts, etc. To augment this incoming flow, fresh air is also pumped through shafts enclosed in staircase wells, or through shafts specially sunk for the purpose.

An earlier method, still employed, works on the exhaust fan principle, between Finsbury Park and Bounds Green on the Cockfosters extension of the Piccadilly Line, three of the numerous working shafts were retained to act as air extraction ducts. Below ground, two galleries and headings connect the shafts to the running tunnels. A later example to assist ventilation is at Notting Hill Gate, where a stairway shaft, no longer used as such, was extended to the roof level of an office block over the station site. All this adaptation and new construction has proved worthwhile, as the older generation of underground travellers would perhaps confirm; especially if they remember positively thrusting their way against the rushes of air which greeted them in passageways as fast moving trains approached a station.

London Transport's intention is to assist passengers at Underground stations with information as much as possible, and to this end, public address facilities are progressively being installed over most parts of the Underground system. Closed circuit television plays its part by enabling station staff to 'oversee' platforms from one station operating room. A closed circuit television system is already installed throughout the Victoria Line, enabling not only the station staff but also the Control Centre at Cobourg Street, Euston, to see what conditions are like at stations. In association with a two-way sound system, station staff can also make announcements when necessary to the public. At some stations, too, there are pushbutton enquiry booths where passengers can obtain information from the station operating room.

Right:
The last of the 1938 stock trains operated on the Bakerloo, and were given an Extra Heavy Overhaul to last them through their final years in service. A 1938 EHO train arrives in the northbound platform at Baker Street. *John Glover*

7
Training, Tickets and Traffic Control

At the London Transport Training Centre it is said that one never stops learning about the railway. This is quite true, and partially explains the presence of middle-aged men at this school for railwaymen; but with regard to the latter, it is perhaps necessary to elucidate by saying that these are men due for promotion and undergoing a course of training for their new responsibilities. At the end of the course comes the decisive examination, and even those few who are unfortunate enough to fail might concede that it is altogether right that the normal way to the top should be the hard way. Millions of people daily entrust their lives to the London Transport railways, and whilst they travel in absolute safety, guarded by devices against every possible human failure, the speedy and regular train services are only maintained by reason of an efficient staff, whose controlling officers know their own job thoroughly, and also a little bit about everyone else's. It can be said that the ladder of promotion rests on the platform, but its top is at dizzy heights; and it is climbable, all the way.

The Training Centre was for many years at Lambeth, over Lambeth North Station on the Bakerloo Line. It became inadequate to deal with a railway system that had not only doubled in size since the Centre was opened in 1920, but had acquired complex equipment never envisaged at that time. The present Centre, light, spacious and fronted with lawns, fits in more with the modern conception of a seat of learning. It has two wings and contains a large assembly hall and main lecture rooms, connected by an administration, study and demonstration block. Its site, previously referred to, lies just to the east of White City Station.

Here the new entrant receives his (or her) training, in the main for operative duties such as junior trainee, railman, booking clerk, guard, etc. Promotional courses are for higher operative duties — driver, signalman, station supervisors etc; special courses are for yet higher posts; and there are too, voluntary classes. There is an air of keenness, comradeship, discipline and relaxation, all mixed in right proportion, about the Centre; and it is perhaps needless to add that all instructors have learned their job thoroughly, not only in theory but in working practice.

They and the students are helped by facilities at the Centre for reproducing almost any situation the trainee is likely to meet on normal railway duties.

Pieces of actual equipment and apparatus at lecturing points are too numerous to mention in detail. One room contains a mock-up of a tunnel section, complete with track, station platform and all the features of a tunnel station. Another contains a booking office complete with ticket issuing machines; others contain an underground car bogie or section of tube car with doors and guard's panel. One big room contains 175ft of model electrified railway track, with 10 miniature 'silver' cars able to be moved about at varying speeds, and under tiny, facsimile signals. This model layout must be interesting to operate in any case; but the operation and instruction are purposeful, aimed to simulate exactly the conditions in full scale working.

Pure lecture rooms may have sheet metal blackboards that take chalk as normal, but to which can also be 'stuck' magnetised apparatus and models of trains. This certainly obviates a lot of repetitive chalking, but one feels it may also have been welcomed by the less artistic instructor. All these features are interesting and informative, but another has been added to provide a sense of realism.

New video monitors have been introduced which are used in conjunction with pre-recorded tapes for many courses. For instance, they enable consideration of historic rail crashes and their influence on London Transport's own safety standards: a record of an operating problem on the Victoria Line, the mistakes that were made and their probable consequences: a Communications Course involving staff role playing passengers on the Centre's mock-up station, whilst the rest of the class watches and recognises the problems — after which the tape is re-played and analysed. A Youth Training Scheme with 26 students working a 52-week course in both the Centre and out on Division is likely to be repeated in future — and to these can be added the 4,200 staff who attend the Centre each year.

We now leave training for practice — in this case, tickets and their issue. It is a far cry from the days when a clerk 'booked' passengers by scrawling their names, fares and destinations on foil and counterfoil of a receipt book, afterwards posting up these copious details on a waybill which he handed to the guard. This was the stage coach system imported into the new world of mechanical locomotion, and almost 150 years ago, in 1836, Thomas Edmondson, stationmaster at Milton on the Newcastle & Carlisle Railway, invented the card ticket, the storage rack and the dating press.

Since those early days, tickets have undergone a succession of changes. On the Underground the 'Scheme' ticket and then the 'Station of origin' ticket reduced variety and made practicable the development of automatic ticket-issuing machines, which print and issue tickets when intending passengers insert the appropriate coin or coins. But the trend on the Underground is toward automation, and therefore quicker and smoother train operation; and if passengers on their way to and from trains are not permitted to move smoothly because of bunching at ticket offices and barriers, they and the train services will not benefit so much from automation. Again, as elsewhere in this book, it is stated that electronics play a principal part in apparatus that, in this instance, performs functions akin to those of the human eye and brain in scrutinising tickets.

Such apparatus enables inward passengers to buy encoded tickets. The tickets will have passed through a rapid printer, equipped with separate printing units, each one with magnetised heads which the ticket actually rubs as it runs beneath them, and is thereby encoded by them with the station of origin, fare, type of ticket and date. London Transport aims eventually to sell nearly all tickets through automatic passenger-operated machines thus fitted; but this is a gradual process. In any case the ticket offices will stock and sell tickets such as those not catered for by the machines.

In brief then, the stage has been reached where passengers have bought their tickets. They then pass through automatic, unmanned ticket gates, where several functions occur, at immense speed so as not to check passengers' progress. A ticket inserted in the front 'wall' is transported past reading heads and delivered halfway through the gate. The front double 'doors' will have opened to let the passengers into the centre, where the exit door to the platform opens and the entrance door closes. All this happens very quickly if the ticket is valid. If for some reason it is not, then the doors will remain closed and the passenger will be directed to the station staff for assistance.

The development of an Underground ticketing system has two parts. First, facilities have to be modernised, to provide much more versatile passenger-operated ticket machines. In future, the ticket office will issue every type of Underground ticket, including through fares to British Rail; details will be keyed into a machine by the clerk. The more common type of passenger-operated machine will issue from a range of the 10 most popular fare values at each station. Change will be given. A multi-fare machine will provide a comprehensive self-service facility to passengers. It will allow passengers to choose their destination and type of ticket (including child, Travelcard etc); it will display the fare, accept coins or notes, and give change.

The second phase involves the ticket control elements, which will eliminate the staffed barrier. Fully automatic entry and exit gates will check all tickets at 60 central area stations. Elsewhere, a system of open stations in the suburban area will rely on spot checks of passengers backed up by a penalty fares system to eliminate fraud.

For some years the whole underground railway system was centrally controlled from an office at Leicester Square, roughly at London's geographical centre. Recently the emphasis has changed and separate line control rooms for individual lines, or groups of lines, linked to the signal regulating system, have been set up. (They are referred to under the heading 'Signalling'.) The separate control offices are, however, linked to a Headquarters controller at London Transport headquarters for information, consultation and so on in matters affecting the Underground as a whole. These highly organised nerve centres sprang from humble origins and can be traced back to the early steam days of the District Railway, when the telegraph office at Earls Court was notified of breakdowns or failures, etc, and from that station orders were issued to maintenance chargehands standing by at various convenient points. Signal fitters at Aldgate East, electrical linesmen at Victoria, and locomotive foremen could thus be summoned to deal with any emergency, whilst a chief inspector stationed at Earls Court was responsible for train working throughout the District system.

With electrification of the District in 1905 came the need for closer control over traffic working, and private telephone lines were laid from a central control office at Earls Court to the important termini, such as Whitechapel and Ealing Broadway. At key points on the route, like Charing Cross, Victoria and Mansion House, telephones were provided that could be plugged into the telegraph circuit on receipt of a telegraphic message 'Come to the telephone' from the controller. Other lines had their control systems, too. The City & South London Railway opened its control office at Moorgate Street on the Euston extension, the Central London Railway control was at Wood Lane, and the joint control for the Bakerloo, Piccadilly & Hampstead lines was at Leicester Square. Control of the Metropolitan Railway was from an office at Baker Street Station.

It was perhaps to be expected that when the various railway systems were grouped under a single authority, all the separate control points would eventually be merged into one. The advantages of having a single control authority, able to visualise the Underground system as a whole, were fairly obvious. Decisive and prompt action could be taken to deal with any interruption to the service at any point, and, if necessary, arrangements could be made with the bus controller or a 'foreign' railway controller to co-operate and ease the passenger situation wherever the interruption had occurred.

8
Acton Overhaul Works and Railway Depots

Acton Works, the central railway overhaul depot in west London, was built in 1922 and officially opened in January 1923. It occupies a large triangle of land, 50 acres, lying south of Acton Town Station on the Piccadilly and District Lines, from which tracks fan out to serve the Works. During its long life there have been alterations and extensions to the Works but up to the present its primary purpose remains unchanged — to provide facilities for heavy overhauling and reconditioning on a periodic basis of all London Transport's railway rolling stock, and to provide a supply of reconditioned wheels and other equipment to the running depots. It follows that with modern equipment and design, the period between overhauls has been lengthened.

During 1984 there were proposals the result of which may mean vehicle overhaul moving in due course to the railway depots, and work at Acton being in consequence confined to the repair of parts; but this is only a possibility. No movement has yet taken place, but the descriptive matter which follows should be read with this in mind.

The works are arranged so that cars for overhaul are first drawn up at a platform alongside the trimming shop, where the seats are removed. The seats are either washed or re-trimmed and then stored ready to go back to the cars after overhaul. Cars can then proceed to the lifting shop where the car body is lifted off its service bogies or trucks by means of a 30 ton overhead traversing crane and placed on special accommodation bogies, which are old bogies built with raised transverse beams so that the body sits much higher off the track than usual, giving additional working space beneath.

After the car bodies are lifted on to accommodation bogies, the service trucks have their traction motors and current collector equipment removed and are drawn by chain into the truck shop. Down one side of this large building is the dismantling track or road, along which the trucks are slowly moved and progressively stripped down to the bare frames.

On the far side of the shop is the truck assembly line and across the wide space between pass all the various components on a series of conveyors. On their journey across the shop, the components are cleaned, inspected and reconditioned or renewed as necessary.

The truck frames themselves are now removed from the line and come

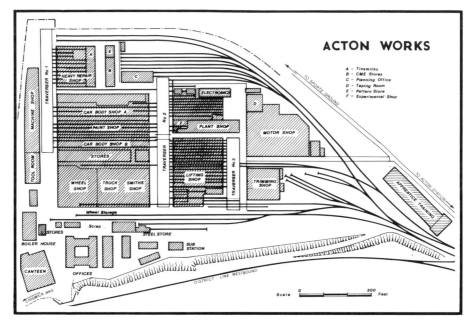

ACTON WORKS

A – Tinsmiths
B – CME Stores
C – Planning Office
D – Taping Room
E – Pattern Store
F – Experimental Shop

under close scrutiny for defects, such as rivets working loose, which may occur under the stress of continued running.

The motor shop overhauls traction motors, compressors, alternators and a variety of other machines such as lift and escalator motors. Motor overhaul is, of course, a specialised business and can vary from superficial attention and cleaning to complete rebuilding from the shaft upwards. Three of the processes involved are the stoving of reconditioned armatures to drive out moisture and ensure good insulation, the banding of armatures to prevent the copper bars from rising due to the high rotating motor speeds, and the armature insulation tests at 2,000V — or double if the armature is rebuilt. These high tension tests are carried out within a special raised enclosure to keep out unauthorised personnel during testing. Modern traction motors use better insulating materials, so the number of machines rewound because of insulation breakdown is decreasing.

The car body overhaul starts when the car is moved from the lifting shop to the blow-out enclosure, where compressed air jets unsettle dust and dirt from the equipment and underframes, while induced draught sucks all this debris away. The car body then travels by traverser to the main car body shop. Compressors and motor alternators are removed to the motor shop, and all electrical and mechanical equipment on the cars, such as brake valves, door engines and traction control equipment are removed for attention at specially equipped benches and then refitted. Overhaul of the car structure and fittings also takes place here. After this process the car body is sent through the paint shop (it must be noted here that modern cars have aluminium exteriors and

120

plastic-faced interiors which require washing only) and then returns to the lifting shop where it is lowered on to its service trucks. Roads with pit facilities are provided for inspection and testing on completed cars. The cars are then coupled into unit formation, the seats refitted, and a final test run performed.

All that is now left of the service trucks on the dismantling road are the pairs of wheels and axles and these are moved to the extreme end of the truck shop, known as the wheel area. Here the wheel assemblies, comprising either wheels, with gear drive mounted directly on the axle, or plain wheels and axles, are subjected to very close examination for wear and faults. Wheel axles, approximately 5in in diameter, sometimes reveal faults during a special testing process. If so, they are tested on an ultrasonic flaw detector. Should there by any suspicion of a crack on an axle, the wheels are pressed off and it is subjected to a test on a magnetic particle tester. In this, fluorescent ink containing particles is sprayed on to the axle, which is then electrified. The particles are thus attracted magnetically to the opposite poles of any crack, which thereupon reveals itself as a black hair line. Overhauled wheel assemblies are conveyed to the assembly line, and then begins the building-up process of the bogie, which continues as the bogie slowly moves along the line in the reverse direction to that in which it entered. The completed trucks are now ready to return to the lifting shop.

Set apart from the 'flow-line' layout is the 300ft long machine shop, with three lines of machines ranging from drills and ordinary lathes to special multi-spindle lathes, automatic, to speed production. The indispensable tool room is under the same roof. Also set apart is the experimental shop, where wooden 'mock-ups' of cars and components are often the half-way stage to innovations and improvements later adopted into active service.

It will be appreciated that only a fraction of the sum total of operations at these works has received attention here. There are operations, of a minute and delicate character, such as one which was shown to the writer some time ago — a piece of car apparatus that would fit into the hand and was vital to efficient running of the railway. The object was a door interlock consisting of a glass bottle, part filled with mercury and containing a pair of electrical contacts. Every sliding door on a train operates one of these devices, tilting the glass bottle when all the doors are closed, so that the mercury bridges the contacts and the door closed circuit is complete, which lights the guard's pilot lamps. The interlock is extremely reliable, there being in excess of three million interlock operations a day on the Underground.

In 1975 a new Apprentice Training Centre was opened adjacent to Acton Works. It accommodates up to 200 trainees and is equipped to cover 20 different trades, providing basic craft training requirements for all London Transport Engineering Departments. With the complexity of training schemes and requirements, the new centralised facilities are an advance on the previous situation, where each department had to arrange its own programmes and facilities. But as always, it is recognised that part of an apprentice's training should include working alongside his senior, on the job.

When Underground lines were built or extended any distance, depots for the stabling of trains were preferably located near to a terminus, on an accessible site not hemmed in by buildings. The Golders Green depot, for example, was built near the terminus, then, of what is now the Northern Line; but at that time (in the early 1900s) it was in open country.

Each line has a main depot and some an ancillary depot. The change in their operations over recent years reflects the fact that depots today are self-sufficient in maintenance of cars up to the standard where only such items as accident damage would demand works attention.

Reference has already been made to the large, comparatively modern depots at West Ruislip and Hainault, just two of nineteen depots and various stabling points that today house the Underground's rolling stock during off-peak hours and, when necessary, undertake servicing.

West Ruislip's variety of work was added to when it took on the job of welding rail into continuous 300ft lengths — work that was previously undertaken at Lillie Bridge Permanent Way Depot (and temporarily elsewhere).

Flash butt welding, as it is known, consists briefly of placing the rail butts, or ends, together, and passing high-tension current through them. The rails are drawn apart slightly during the operation to create an arc, and when this has been done a few times the butt becomes so hot and soft that when pressed tightly together they fuse into one. This is a simplified description of the operation. A technical description would prolong it beyond the scope of this book.

Speaking of 300ft lengths of rail conjures a vision of transport difficulties; but it can be said that rail welded into these lengths is now used extensively, and is being conveyed to the very furthest limits of the system. The difficulty of transporting 300ft continuous lengths of rail is not so great as might be imagined. A train of specially designed wagons is made up, and the long rails rest on these, each lying between upright iron pegs which prevent any lateral movement. The rail lengths are flexible enough to adapt themselves to whatever curve the train negotiates, and to assume their original shape when the train straightens out. It is most interesting to watch the serpentine progress of such a train.

A device that speeded rail laying is named the 'Thimble' although it appears to be used more like a threader. In brief it is a roller-mounted device which is hoisted by a crane at the point where laying is to commence. The end of a 300ft off-loaded length of rail is jacked up, and on to it is threaded the thimble. The crane is then reversed and travels slowly backwards over the rail, feeding it through the thimble, the jib being so positioned as to drop the rail in the chairs awaiting it. Conductor rail can similarly be placed on its insulators, aided and guided where necessary by men with bars.

Loading rails from the track site has also been speeded up by the introduction of a specially constructed train. Past practice when removing 300ft lengths of rail from the track was to cut them up and load them piece-meal but the new train, hauled by battery locomotive, can load up to 18 such rails whole, as it were. The new procedure, described simply, is to winch up the end of the rail to be removed, guide it over a roller in a hinged frame on to the rear wagon and then propel the whole train *under* the rail until the last 20ft overhangs the roller. This is then hauled on by the winch.

One wonders how the rail expansion problem is overcome when laying rails of such lengths, especially since 300ft is nothing like the limit for rail laid without the usual 'breathing' joint. Quite long stretches of welded running rail are laid, and the joint between lengths is made by what is known as the machined joint, which is fishplated and absolutely tight.

In the open, where expansion is far greater than in tunnel, a switch rail is placed every half mile of track at a joint. The tapered end of a long running rail is laid against it so that it can slide backwards or forwards for adjustment whilst still maintaining the correct gauge.

On the stretch of line from Leytonstone to Newbury Park, 3½ miles in length, there is not one ordinary joint, but only insulating joints and machined joints allowing for no expansion; but it must be remembered that practically all this stretch is in tunnel, where variations in temperature are not of great moment.

Rail lengths must vary to suit particular jobs, and are determined by the position of block joints for track circuiting, or by the curvature or gradient of the line affected. Running rails of 60ft and 90ft were used on the tunnel sections of the Cockfosters extension, and these were jointed by 18in fishplates. On the north-east extension of the Central Line, 60ft rails were welded into continuous 300ft lengths, the work being done at various depots and on site. In the latter case a portable flush butt-welding machine was used, and subsequently the joint and rail ends were normalised or returned to their original state of toughness by placing over them a portable normalising oven. Welding is also employed to join conductor rail lengths, in these instances gaps are left every 800yd.

Upminster Depot, brought into full service in 1959, is one of the system's largest. It accommodates 34 eight-car trains on its extensive network of sidings and roads; and as an aid to movement into and out of the former, a system of centralised control was introduced. Points are power-operated and controlled by switches in a control tower, the duty man there being able to give instructions to drivers through small trackside loudspeakers, and to hear a driver when he replies at ordinary speech level into his microphone. Among other innovations at that time were the installation of two-way radio apparatus for use by depot-employed shunters, new types of train-washing apparatus and powerful floodlighting over the whole operating area.

9
The Victoria Line

Towards the end of World War 2, thoughts turned to postwar reconstruction, and led eventually to the London Plan Working Party Report, published in 1949.

The proposals were vast in conception and could not have envisaged the enormous growth of motor transport in the 40 years between then and now — but even so, several of the Working Party's plans were sound enough to have been wholly or partly implemented, even though they needed some adaptation; and some may yet serve as a guide to future development. The reader may judge for himself, as the proposals are outlined as follows:

New railways in tube would be divided into two types, urban, of existing tube dimensions, and outer suburban of 17ft diameter to take main line rolling stock. The urban type would, with numerous stops, run intensive services of up to 40 trains per hour, whilst the outer suburban would work at a density of about 25 trains per hour.

Some of the proposals are summarised thus:

(A) Electrification of the suburban lines from King's Cross to Hitchin, including the Hertford Loop, and of the lines from St Pancras to Luton or St Albans.

(B) A new urban tube from the Tottenham and Walthamstow areas via Finsbury Park, King's Cross, Euston, Oxford Circus, Green Park, Victoria, Vauxhall, Stockwell, Brixton and Streatham to East Croydon. This tube was considered as Priority.

(C) Electrification of the suburban lines from Chingford and Enfield Town and a new urban tube to connect these services at Hackney Downs to Liverpool Street, Bank, Ludgate Circus, Aldwych, Trafalgar Square and Victoria.

(D) Electrification of Eastern Region's Tilbury and Southend line into Fenchurch Street, these services to be continued in tube to the Bank and Waterloo.

(E) Electrification of Eastern Region's Cambridge line from Bishops Stortford, including the reopening of the Churchbury Loop, as well as the Hertford East and Chingford branches.

All of these have now been wholly or partly implemented in a recognisable form, albeit many years later in some cases. Schemes which were not adopted included:

(F) A new tube extending the Holborn-Aldwych tube to Camberwell and Crystal Palace.

(G) Providing East and South East London with a tube railway by extending the Northern City Line from Moorgate to Woolwich and Plumstead.

(H) Linking certain outer suburban rail passenger services north of the Thames with those to the south, via cross-town railways in 17ft diameter tube to take main line stock. This will in part be met by reopening the Farringdon-Blackfriars link.

The implementation of proposal B (in truncated form as the Victoria Line) gave London its first completely new underground railway in 62 years, the one before it being the 'Hampstead Tube', opened in 1907.

Although a British Transport Commission Private Bill was introduced in Parliament in 1955, and statutory powers obtained for the construction of 11½ miles of tube railway from Victoria to Walthamstow obtained subsequently, there followed several years of intensive investigation, including aerial survey of the route and sinking about 70 exploratory boreholes. During this time it was decided that a portion of tunnel along the proposed route be excavated and lined by new methods as a preliminary, to gain practical experience.

Work began on a mile stretch of experimental tunnel north of Finsbury Park in January 1960 and was completed in July of the following year. It provided valuable data on tunnelling through London clay, which would be encountered along most of the line's route; on work with the mechanical 'drum-digger' shield (previously referred to) and on techniques for expanding tunnel linings against clay immediately after the erection of each ring, thereby obviating the time-wasting job of injecting concrete grout in the cavities left after normal lining. The experimental tunnel concrete lining segments were cast with convex and concave edges to form knuckle joints, and the rings were finally expanded by wedges, the last being ram-driven at pressure. Cast iron lining segments were somewhat similar in finished shape, and rings of segments were expanded by jacking, the pressure being locked in by taper packings. This method of lining had been given a trial as early as 1958, when a short length of 14ft diameter water tunnel for a generating station for the Central Electricity Generating Board was lined by this method experimentally. Its reliability was demonstrated on a larger scale in the experimental tube tunnel, and in the event was adopted for construction of the actual Victoria Line tunnel.

All this was in preparation for what may well be considered the most complicated railway construction work in any city in the world. In August 1962 Government finally approved construction of the Victoria Line, agreeing to advance the estimated £56million capital cost as a loan, and within a few months the first actual construction began on the new line.

The railway initially had its southern terminus at Victoria, Southern Region, BR and proceeded thence via the following stations: Green Park, Oxford Circus, Warren Street, Euston, King's Cross & St Pancras, Highbury & Islington, Finsbury Park, Seven Sisters, Tottenham Hale, Blackhorse Road, to Hoe Street (Walthamstow Central), its north-eastern terminus.

It was originally intended to continue another ¾-mile to Wood Street (Eastern Region), where cross-platform exchange would have been provided with the latter's services to Highams Park and Chingford. The introduction by BR of high-voltage traction current by overhead transmission at its Wood Street station, however, caused London Transport to alter its plan for the new railway.

The main objects of the Victoria Line were to provide a more direct route to the City and West End from the north-eastern suburbs and to lessen congestion of the Piccadilly and District Lines.

General principles aimed at in building the actual tube were: an avoidance of curves sharper than 20 chains radius; stations built on a hump or saw-tooth profile (giving a falling gradient away from the station and a rising gradient approaching it); a tunnel diameter sufficient to minimise air resistance, and the line to be as straight as possible between any two points. These ideals were followed as closely as possible during the task of fitting the tube, as it were, into a mazelike pattern of existing stations, tunnels and sewers.

In September 1966 the tremendous job of excavating the Victoria Line's twin tunnels by the shield method was completed. During 35 months it had involved 44 different tunnel drives starting from 21 shafts sunk for that purpose, the last drive breaking through an already completed tunnel section near King's Cross. There remained only a few short sections of running tunnel to be excavated without the use of a shield.

The surface work included building 12 ventilating fan houses, nine electrical substations, and the Northumberland Park train depot. It was finally opened throughout the whole length for passenger traffic, from Walthamstow to Victoria, in March 1969, and took 6½ years to build from start to finish. And to illustrate the magnitude of the job underground, more than two miles of platform tunnel for the 12 stations, over 40 escalator shafts, numerous subways, six sidings, and new and enlarged ticket halls were excavated.

All the Victoria Line is in tunnel, and a large part of it was driven beneath the central area of London that was already, as has been said, honeycombed with ducts, passageways, shafts, sub-surface railways, deep tubes and sewers, large and small.

At Victoria, the ticket hall for both the Victoria and District Lines was sited under an existing forecourt of the main line station, with access to both lines, and direct access between the two lines themselves. The Victoria Line's

126

platforms lie 59ft below the new ticket hall; and beyond, to the south, there were four tube sidings, two of which were later continued as the Brixton extension.

The main line station was largely built over a filled-in canal basin, presumably part of the Chelsea Waterworks reservoir or cut, recorded as having been built there in the 18th century. It was necessary to stabilise part of the thick stratum of water-bearing sand and gravel, to permit deep mining beneath it, by injecting chemicals through a large number of narrow pipes driven 35ft into the gravel over the affected area to harden it.

A large part of the land south of Victoria down to the Thames was ancient low drainage ground, referred to as early as the year 951 as Bulinga Fen, into which the Tyburn may have drained. This once-open river is now non-existent or reduced to a subterranean trickle, but it is very roughly beneath and along its former line that the Victoria tube runs northward to cross deep under the Mall opposite Queen Victoria Memorial, and under Green Park at about 75ft to Green Park station.

The Victoria Line station here lies just to the west and above the Piccadilly Line station, connected to the latter by a subway, and to the new ticket hall by a bank of three escalators. From Green Park the line, having crossed the Piccadilly Line roughly at right angles, runs north again beneath Mayfair to Oxford Circus, for interchange with the Bakerloo and Central Lines. It has climbed steadily to follow the land contour rising from the Thames, but is still about 70ft below the surface.

Tunnelling here was a major job, as the tubes swing out to flank the Bakerloo on each side, thus providing the ideal cross-platform interchange. Building this composite station below ground took longer than any other station building along the line: and the only visible surface evidence of the day and night activity going on below was the 600 ton steel 'umbrella' bridging the whole of Oxford Circus itself, which carried all the street traffic 3ft 6in above the former street level. Below the Circus is a large circular ticket hall and below that are five new escalator shafts, separate Victoria Line station tunnels, subways, passages and concourses linking with the Bakerloo, and the Central running at right angles at low level. No person, of course, ever sees the whole of this underground complex at one time, and the only simile the writer can bring to mind is that of an oil refinery's steel towers and pipes magnified, laid sideways in the ground and buried.

At this station the engineers were faced with an unusually intricate task — that of underpinning part of Peter Robinson's store, and transferring the load from its foundations to the southbound Victoria Line Station tunnel. Below the third basement, the building's columns were under-pinned with massive pre-stressed concrete, the bottom layer cast in weaker concrete. Later, the tunnel shield drove beneath a saddle shape cut in the base of the concrete, and finally the station tunnel segments were expanded by jacks to produce in the ground the necessary stresses.

The line continues north from Oxford Circus station, cutting diagonally across a grid pattern of streets above to Warren Street, at the junction of Euston Road and Tottenham Court Road. Along the route the northbound running tunnel is made to roll over the south-bound tunnel, and continues thus to Warren Street, about 90ft down, where new escalators connect the Victoria Line with the existing escalators for the Northern Line at an intermediate landing level 50ft below street level. Beyond Warren Street the tunnels swing north-east to Euston, another deep level underground complex which provides interconnection between the British Railways terminal station above, and both the City (via Bank) and West End branches of the Northern Line. The reversed tunnels emerge into a combined, one level, double-island Euston station with the northbound tunnel on the right and the southbound on the left. Across their respective platforms are the northbound City branch trains to Camden Town and the southbound City trains to King's Cross. These platforms are unusual in that trains run in opposite directions on each side of them. Pedestrian subways give access to Northern Line West End branch trains.

The line rises gradually then to King's Cross, 1½ miles from Oxford Circus. A description of the fairly recent reconstruction of King's Cross underground station and the British Railways 'widened lines' as given earlier in this book provides some idea of the congested maze of tunnels and the like through which the Victoria Line tunnels had to be threaded and a new tube station positioned.

A complicating feature not mentioned earlier was the brick arch of the Midland Curve tunnel then used by BR diesel trains, which had to be removed, and replaced by a new structure of reinforced concrete so as to provide room for a peripheral subway. Lower down, part of the Victoria Line's station tunnel crown is positioned a few feet below the foundations of the Midland Curve and Circle Line tunnels. As these are in brick with either no inverts, or inverts of varying depth, an extra robust tunnel shield was employed here to exert great pressure on the ground at its working face during excavation. Finally, extra heavy steel tunnel lining was expanded against the ground by powerful jacks and steel wedges, so as to maintain at all times equilibrium of ground stresses and prevent settlement of the brick tunnel foundations.

King's Cross is the only 'four-tier' station on the Underground system. The whole of the work here, including line and station construction and equipping, took roughly 3½ years. Beyond this station the tunnels curve and ascend to follow the rising ground to Highbury & Islington, providing interchange there with what was the Northern City (Moorgate) line and is now the BR Inner Suburban line.

About half-way along this 1½ mile stretch the running tunnels were made to roll back, southbound over northbound, to the normal positions they occupy for the remainder of the route. The old station, dating from 1904, was extensively rebuilt below ground and its surface building resited in what was the forecourt of the London Midland Region's Highbury & Islington Station. As a result of the reconstruction below ground, the former northbound Northern City platform became the Victoria Line southbound platform, the former line having been diverted slightly, through a newly driven tunnel, to a new platform. The other side of this platform accommodates the northbound Victoria Line. Thus there is cross-platform 'directional' interchange between the two lines and above-ground connection with the London Midland Region surface line.

The running tunnels continue another mile to Finsbury Park, where the old Great Northern & City Line and the Piccadilly Line's stations, opened in 1904 and 1906 respectively, were literally transformed to accommodate the modern tube. The below ground works here involved building step-plate junctions around tunnels (whilst trains continued to operate); building underground crossovers, and ultimately switching trains from old lines to new. The transformation resulted in southbound Piccadilly and Victoria Line trains using the old Northern City Line's once-terminal station, and northbound trains of the same lines using the Piccadilly station, with same-level interchange between southbound Victoria Line and Piccadilly trains and between northbound trains on the two lines.

This brings us back to the steel skeleton framework on the surface at Finsbury Park. When referring earlier in this book to the old Great Northern & City Line, plans were mentioned for extending this up and over the bridge structure at Finsbury Park (High Level) to High Barnet and Alexandra Palace. This was ruled out subsequently, but the bygone planners' dreams were in the event finally realised, in so far as rolling stock of main line dimensions did in fact roll through the 16ft tunnels from Moorgate to Hertfordshire, but not until 1976. The Victoria tube tunnels run north-east descending steadily to Seven Sisters; at 1.96 miles this became the longest stretch of railway underground on the system without an intermediate station. Seven Sisters is interchange for electric surface trains between Liverpool Street and Enfield/Hertford, and also for bus passengers. There are two separate ticket halls, one near the Tottenham High Road entrance, and the other, in Seven Sisters Road, connected with the Eastern Region surface station. The halls are connected to the tube platforms 60ft below ground by escalators and stairs.

The station has three tracks, the centre one leaving the eastbound track just west of the station and leading subsequently to the Northumberland Park Train Depot. The outer ones are the east and westbound tracks, the latter receiving the other track from the train depot at a point just east of the station. The two depot tracks swing northward in tunnel for about ½-mile, then rise through a cutting to parallel the main Eastern Region Cambridge/Liverpool Street line until they fan out into the depot sidings. Four tracks continue into the large depot itself, two to pass the train washing plant, and the other two for trains going into or coming out of service. The depot building, similar to, but larger than the Upminster Depot described herein, accommodates a full-length tube train on each of its 12 tracks. Here also London Transport has covered sidings, capable of stabling two trains on each of the 11 sidings.

The tube running tunnels continue north-east, descending along a distance of a mile to the Lea Valley and Tottenham Hale, where the underground station connects with the Eastern Region station on the Cambridge line. From here the tube ascends and swings eastward to continue a mile to Blackhorse Road, and another 2/3 mile to the terminus, Walthamstow Central, both stations connecting with BR Eastern Region trains.

The Victoria Line, from beyond Finsbury Park (the actual Park) to Walthamstow, broke virgin ground for underground railways. The route it takes from Tottenham follows in fact the old road once used principally by cyclists over the River Lea, and then along with ancient electric trams through misty marsh and reservoir to glorious Epping Forest. The Great Eastern Railway opened up Walthamstow to development with steam trains 90 years ago, but the Victoria Line had no such development aspirations. Instead it aimed to attract traffic from this built-up area, and from the north-eastern suburbs beyond, by interchange with the surface lines.

All this northern end of the line's running tunnels were driven through blue clay, as was part of the southern end, excavated by shield and rotary cutters to bite into the clay, in the manner described in an earlier chapter. Tunnelling began from a working site in Ferry Lane, Tottenham, where a 46ft shaft was sunk. From its foot a horizontal shaft was driven a short distance to the line of the running tunnel, where a chamber was excavated for the running tunnel shield to be assembled. One of the vertical shafts along the route was utilised subsequently to house a substation and fan house. For the larger diameter station tunnels and for a crossover at Walthamstow the tunnel lining is in cast iron segment form, and the running tunnels in concrete segments. Much of the southern end of the Victoria Line's running tunnels were lined with cast iron segments, some of the new design similar to those used in the experimental tunnel, but for water-bearing and other 'difficult' ground encountered along the route, conventional bolted cast iron segments were used.

Of the mass of 'furnishing' for the line, only the basic features can be mentioned here, thus: Jarrah wood sleepers, virtually indestructible, concreted into the tunnel roadbed; 300ft lengths of running rail welded as such at the Northumberland Park Depot and fed in from there; and a narrow concrete shelf or platform fixed to the tunnel walls at about platform height to contain the noise of wheel on rail.

The power supply for the Victoria Line comes primarily from Lots Road and Greenwich, stepped down from 22kV to 11kV in the Cobourg Street switch-house, and thence fed to nine substations supply the line between

130

Walthamstow and Victoria. (The Brixton extension supply reaches it via substations at Stockwell and Brixton.) The main electrical control room for the whole line is at Manor House.

The term 'automation' as applied to the Victoria Line is not limited to the operation of its trains. It embraces signalling, passenger movement (automatic control of station entrances and exits), fare collection and station supervision,

Automatic signalling and routeing of trains to predetermined schedules, where train movement can be controlled throughout the day at junctions, sidings, terminals and entrances to car depots, together with advance describing of trains' destinations for display at stations, are already a fully automated feature on other sections of the Underground system as well as on the Victoria Line. Automatic Train Operation, however, is important enough to call for some special attention.

Under non-automatic conditions the train driver applies power to the motors, cuts it off or applies the brakes as dictated by track conditions and the state of signals. Under automatic conditions the human element is almost entirely cut out and the train is under a dual system of control. The most important system safeguards the train (ie puts it under the control of safety signals) by employing an inductive pick-up to receive continuous coded signals from the track, and equipment to interpret and act upon these signals. This is the safety signalling system. The other, the 'driver command' system, receives impulses at 'spots' along the track. These cause power to be cut off for coasting, brakes to be applied, etc, and a series of them controls the stopping of trains in the station platforms.

In somewhat more detail, the safety signalling codes are formed by current from the mains supply. In a relay room this current is interrupted into codes by the action of pendulums operating electronic switches. One pendulum, swinging 180 times a minute, produces a '180' impulse code. A faster swinging pendulum produces a '420' impulse code. This coded signal current is fed into the running rails (divided into sections by insulated joints) passing along one rail, through the wheels and axles at the front of the train, and then back by the other rail. Coils mounted on the front of the train are affected by the code in the rails and a signal is passed to the train equipment, amplified, and recognised by electrical circuits responding only to an appropriate code frequency. A '180' code indicates that the train is safe to proceed at 22mph and it is made to conform to this speed by a mechanical governor, actuated by the train wheels, that ensures this speed is not exceeded whilst the '180 code' is being received. A '420' code indicates that the train may proceed at full speed. While one of these safety signal codes is being received by the train, current from the train battery holds an emergency brake valve in the closed position. If the code should cease to be picked up by the train the current would be cut off the brake valve and an emergency application of brakes would result.

131

This is the safety signalling part of automatic train operation. The other part is described as 'automatic driver signal command'. These commands are also derived from current fed into the track, but in this case only into short sections or 'spots' (10ft) of one running rail. An electronic generator produces current of a special frequency which is obeyed by equipment on the trains. Current at 100 cycles per second equals 1mph permitted to the trains; at 1,000 cycles it equals 10mph, and at 3,000 cycles, 30mph. One of the main purposes of the driver command equipment is to apply the brakes to stop the train accurately in the station, and careful calculations are made to enable command spots to be positioned along the track at the appropriate positions.

The command signal frequency, picked up by an inductive coil on the train, is counted by an electronic counter and the frequency compared with the frequency produced by a speedometer generator on the train. As a result of comparing the frequencies, electrical circuits regulate the train's progress to the correct predetermined speed required, by causing brake application or release. This occurs at station approaches, but there are also command spots along the line where the train has reached sufficient speed to allow it to coast to the next station. The frequency at these spots, 15,000 cycles per second, is outside the speed range of the train and is recognised by a special circuit, which issues a command to cut the motors.

For example, in operation a train may be imagined as having left one station, and some distance ahead in the next station a train is standing. Between the trains would be a '420' signal coded section (unrestricted speed), then a '180' section (restriction to 22mph) and ahead of that a 'No code' section, to safeguard the rearward train from approaching too close to the stationary train. Presuming this latter train had moved off, leaving, again for example, an unoccupied station and a clear and straightforward run ahead of the rearward train, that train would be able to proceed under '420' signal code to a 15,000 cycle command spot, where current would be cut automatically from the motors and the train would coast to the first of the command spots at the next station approach. Here it would pass command spots at 3,000, 2,500, 2,000, 1,500 and 1,000 cycles/sec, each one commanding a gradual speed reduction of 30mph through 25, 20, 15 and 10mph to a final halt. This would be at a predetermined platform stop, which the train would approach and stop at in a gradual braking curve, regardless of its load at the time.

In 1964 and later in 1968, just before the initial opening of the Victoria Line, the writer was privileged to ride on an automatically operated train. Both trips were in the nature of test runs, the first on the Teito Rapid Transit line in Tokyo and the second on the Central Line's Woodford-Hainault branch. On both occasions these different ATO systems worked perfectly, to the untrained observer and apparently to the expert. The Victoria Line's automatic trains have been carrying passengers and operating with quiet efficiency ever since.

Earlier on, in 1962, District Line rolling stock was equipped with automatic apparatus and ran experimentally on a mile stretch of test track between South Ealing and Acton Town; and on 8 April 1963 a train on a routine trip from Ealing Common to Upminster was switched from manual to automatic operation over a stretch of equipped track between Stamford Brook and Ravenscourt Park.

In 1967 work began on the Victoria Line to extend it 3½ miles southward in tube to Brixton. Twin tunnels driven under the Thames (the first for 40 years) lead to Vauxhall station, via Pimlico station on the north bank. Stockwell station, already served by the Northern Line comes next, and provides same-level interchange with the latter. Brixton Station is the terminus serving a particularly densely populated area of South London. There were thus three new stations added to the Underground, although Pimlico was not opened until a few months after the extension became operative in July 1971. The additional stations, like all those on the Victoria Line, have a distinction exclusive to that line. The walls are ornamented with a motif, individual to each station, illustrating some local association. The completed Victoria Line was, at its opening, described as the world's most highly automated underground railway. The southern extension, built at the then cost of £21millions — met as to 75% by the Government and 25% by the Greater London Council — brought for the first time one-man automatically operated trains south of the river. It made possible the quickest journey time for any form of public transport from Brixton to Walthamstow, 14 miles in 32 minutes. The average service speed of 43mph for an urban underground railway is fast by any standard.

The twin tunnels to Brixton were driven at a depth of just over 60ft south of Victoria, crossing at the lowest point 24ft under the Thames river bed, and continuing thence to Brixton at depths varying between 40 and 50ft. Fortunately the project was authorised in time to ensure continuity of employment for some of the highly specialised teams of enginers and others who were assembled to build and equip the Victoria-Walthamstow line.

Left:
More repair work is to be undertaken in line depots. 1972 Mk II stock is seen prepared for attention at Neasden.
John Glover

10
Heathrow Extension, Jubilee Line and Docklands

On 16 December 1977 the Queen rode in a tube train from Hounslow to Heathrow Central, and thus inaugurated the Piccadilly Heathrow extension services. The extension tracks run westward 3½ miles from Hounslow West, first on the surface to cross the River Crane and then at sub-surface in a single box-section tunnel built by the cut and cover method, to Hatton Cross. Just beyond this station the tracks descend into twin tunnels 3.81m (12ft 6in) in diameter lined with concrete rings, and continue at deep level beneath the airport runways to a much larger 9.5m (31ft 2in) tunnel that houses the crossover outside Heathrow Central Station. This portion lies under water-bearing gravel and had to be built under compressed air conditions. The crossover allows trains to leave and to arrive at both the station platforms, which lie 44ft below the surface.

When the world's busiest international airport, London's Heathrow, was connected to the Piccadilly Line, it became the first such airport to be linked to a metropolitan underground system. Heathrow began in 1929 as the small Great Western Aerodrome, with only grass runways used for experimental test flying. During World War II the site was chosen as a base for the Royal Air Force long-range transport flights, and by 1945 military aircraft were taking off from its only constructed runway (at that time). Civilian flying was introduced when the first airlines came to the aerodrome, using converted military aircraft for their flights: and by then, as London's new airport, it was officially opened in May 1946.

Air travel then was so much in its infancy that the actual port functioned for several years with not much more than a collection of tents serving as Custom Office and Waiting Room etc; but even then it attracted a sight-seeing public who were allowed into a fenced-off grass enclosure. The build-up of traffic from then on was rapid, so much so that within 10 years, aviation and railway officials were talking about a rail link to the airport. Both surface and elevated monorail systems were considered, as well as the Underground. The link by Underground was eventually decided upon (although a surface rail connection is still a possibility), only because imaginative planners foresaw air travel of the future as something which would largely supersede ocean travel, and be used by ordinary people in their millions. For London the familiar Underground would, they predicted, offer the best facilities for intensive passenger traffic to and from its centre and suburbs — and so ultimately the link was made.

Heathrow Central, subsequently renamed Heathrow Terminals 1, 2, 3 is located , as near as makes no odds, beneath the airport's dead centre. To reach the huge sunken concrete box, 119m long and 23m wide, in which it is housed, tunnels had obviously to be driven under the runways. In a box at lowest level are the station platforms served by twin rail tracks. Above them is a mezzanine floor containing staff rooms and equipment; above that is the concourse and ticket hall and finally, at surface level, the toilet block and station entrance. The roof in parts is two metres thick to allow for any future over-building. Subways containing long, moving walkways lead from the concourse to the three airport terminals, so travellers arriving or departing by Underground move below-ground normally, from station to terminal and vice versa.

The station, and therefore the large concourse, being the first of its kind in the world, has several unique features. There is a comprehensive information centre plus the usual ticket-vending machines, and one special multi-fare machine, and — another 'first', — an illuminated journey planner. To any enquirer pushing one of its many buttons it displays in colour the best suggested route by Underground to any of its stations, and augments this with a 'print-out' description in English, French and German!

It was suggested at one time that should air traffic increase to warrant building a new Terminal 4, the latter might be connected with Heathrow's intermediate station, Hatton Cross, by a moving walkway-subway. This was the situation in 1980. Since then, a major development at the airport has taken place. Regarding airport noise, a new generation of aircraft with quieter engines has eased the problem although air traffic has increased — and to cope with this further problem the Airport authority consulted advisers, amongst whom was London Transport. The outcome was a decision to build a new terminal complex, No 4, on a site about a mile southeast of Heathrow Terminals 1, 2, 3 underground station, just inside the airport's southern perimeter. Air traffic at the existing terminals handling domestic, European and intercontinental flights, already considerable, would predictably outgrow their capacity in the future and need a fourth terminal to supplement the airport's total capacity.

The suggested subway-walkway project was eventually abandoned in favour of a western underground extension of the Piccadilly Line from Hatton Cross in the form of a single-track loop, to serve first the new Terminal 4, then Heathrow Terminals 1, 2, 3 and finally back to Hatton Cross, thence eastward to London. The new (and huge) Air Terminal 4 was expected to open in 1986. Its airside concourse is 680 metres (approaching ½ mile) long: and below ground, close to the southward facing side is the Underground station. Such a vast airport complex, whose own future passenger flow is an estimated eight millions per annum, demands to be adequately served by its

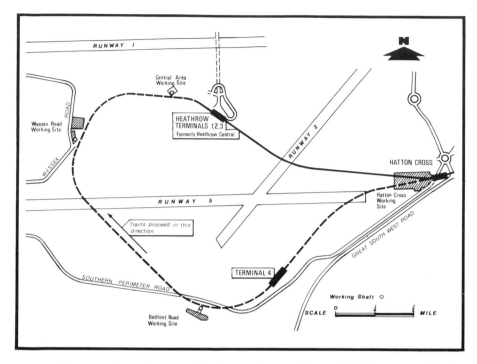

own underground station as well as by surface traffic, and this is catered for in the overall plan. The British Airports Authority (BAA) is responsible not only for building the surface complex but also for building the Underground station, to London Transport's design. The latter is responsible for the railway tunnelling costing an estimated £20 millions in total: which sum is inclusive of railway signalling, track and other equipment.

This loop line, which describes a rough circle beneath and within the airport area, totals about 3¾ miles in length, all of which is in new tunnel. Piccadilly Line trains will thus continue south-eastward from Hatton Cross to Terminal 4 station, thence in a half-circle towards Terminals 1, 2, 3 where they will enter either one of the two original over run tunnels and continue eastward, but will use only one of the two existing tracks beyond the station to Hatton Cross. The other track will be used as and when required — for local movement for instance. The new single-track tunnel was constructed in three sections; for just over ¾-mile from a shaft near Hatton Cross station on to Terminal 4 station, and from another shaft at Wessex Road (at the airport's western end) for two miles southeast back to Terminal 4 station, and about one mile (including the links to both over run tunnels) northeast to Heathrow Terminals 1, 2, 3.

It seems proper here to give space to the work involved as the project comprises not only an extension to the Piccadilly Line likely to grow in importance, but it has several unusual features that have led to the solving of new problems. To begin with, excavations just west of Hatton Cross station had to take place almost directly beneath the flight path of aircraft. No component part such as lifting gear and stacked material had to rise above a certain level, to exceed which would have created radar interference and thus affected aircraft in flight. So the large working area had first to be made into a kind of shallow pit, and in a deep trench below that a new rail junction, plus a ¼-mile section of tunnel had to be built and afterwards covered in.

The new Hatton Cross junction was built within a concrete sub-surface formation, necessitating careful demolition of the original box. Then follows a descending section of tunnel with cast-iron lining, built in trench and afterwards backfilled. A tunnelling shield, for which a chamber had first to be constructed in open excavation, was used to drive the running tunnel, as were two other shields (all three thrust forward into London clay at depths down to 17 metres below ground by powerful hydraulic rams), working from the Wessex Road site. Other less powerful rams were used to push home the wedge sections of the expanded tunnel lining.

Tunnel face cutting within the circular shields was by apparatus known as boom cutters and the core of spoil removed rearward by conveyors. Eventually this reached the surface up inclined drift tunnels. Most of the running tunnel was lined with precast concrete rings, made in a local factory set up for the purpose. Where the new single-track tunnel divides to link with the two original over run tunnels, a step-plate junction was constructed. Flat-bottomed welded rail on pre-stressed concrete sleepers form the new track and are the first so employed in deep Tube sections of the Underground system. And mainly to reduce noise, sleepers on part of the new track rest on experimental rubber-like 'boots'. To ventilate the loop, two air shafts were sunk to supplement the existing shaft at the airport centre.

London's second new underground railway is the Jubilee Line. This statement is true in essence although the Jubilee Line takes over an existing 17.7km (11-mile) stretch of Bakerloo Line from Baker Street to Stanmore.

Stage I of the Jubilee Line was sanctioned by Government in 1971, who realised the need for a new tube to provide access to the West End, and later the City, from north-west London. Equally important was the fact that the Bakerloo Line from Baker Street to Oxford Circus, perhaps surprisingly, was the most heavily used section of the whole Underground network during peak hours, and needed to be relieved of much of its overcrowding. The situation was brought about by the funnelling of two Bakerloo lines, the Queens Park and Stanmore branches, into one at Baker Street. They are now separate lines. Bakerloo and Jubilee. Construction work on Stage I, comprising a new tube from Baker Street via Bond Street and Green Park to Trafalgar Square (re-named Charing Cross) began in February 1972.

Separating the Bakerloo lines at Baker Street, deep underground, so that the Queens Park branch would have its own two platforms and the Stanmore branch (becoming the Jubilee Line) would also have its two platforms, with all four interconnecting in one station, presented problems. Their solution resulted in a neat and compact station layout, but a difficult one to describe adequately with confusing.

Suffice to say here that it involved building two new step-plate junctions, one just to the south of the station and one 1,000ft to the north about 50ft below Marylebone main line station. Additionally a new station tunnel and a new running tunnel were driven on the north side of the existing southbound Stanmore platform. The end result is that this latter becomes the southbound Jubilee Line platform, and the new station tunnel and platform becomes the northbound Jubilee tunnel and platform. To achieve this, the northbound Jubilee running tunnel had to be made to roll over the southbound tunnel both north and south of the station, which means that the new line's running in the station is the reverse of that of the Bakerloo Line.

The actual construction of the step-plate junctions (a term derived from the reduction in steps of large to small diameter tunnel linings) had as perhaps expected, to be done without interfering with the lines' normal running. Most of the work, such as building large diameter junction tunnels around existing 12ft tunnels, was done during normal service hours, but that of dismantling the old inner tunnel linings and connecting the trackwork had to be concentrated into the four to five hours 'shut-down' at night — a procedure already described in a previous chapter.

At depths of between 20 and 40m (70-140ft) the new twin tunnels run south and east for nearly 4½km (about three miles) from Baker Street to Charing Cross. The first station is Bond Street, where only 7ft separates the station tunnel from a smaller one above, carrying driverless Post Office mail trains between Paddington and Whitechapel. In anticipation of eight million more passengers a year, Bond Street has had its sub-surface booking hall enlarged threefold. This meant excavating below the pavement and street outside, to do which and keep traffic moving, an immense temporary steel deck or 'umbrella' 230ft long was built to carry traffic and pedestrians, whilst men worked below. The umbrella was removed in 1975. The Jubilee Line also passes below the Central Line here, to which it is connected by draught relief tunnels and passageways for interchanging passengers.

From Bond Street the line veers south-east to Green Park station. It passes below both the Piccadilly and Victoria lines to reach the new station platforms, just east of and below the latter's station. There is interconnection between all three lines, aided by new passageways and escalators as at Bond Street. The Jubilee Line continues at a depth of about 90ft to the third and final station in Stage I of the project at Charing Cross.

Locating and building this station was a major engineering project. First the Strand section of the Northern Line station had to be closed, as a shaft for a bank of three new escalators had to be driven diagonally through the lift shaft serving that station. The new Charing Cross incorporates the Trafalgar Square Bakerloo station with the new Jubilee Line station and with the old

Strand Northern Line, all being interconnected either by stairways or escalators. The Jubilee Line here runs diagonally under the Bakerloo and also, at right angles, under the Northern Line, its running tunnels having meanwhile curved eastward from Green Park.

An umbrella construction was also needed here, under the Charing Cross BR Southern Region station forecourt. Of interest perhaps to the historian is the Queen Eleanor memorial in the forecourt. Its 300 ton weight had to be eased up to allow it to be underpinned whilst work went on building the new ticket hall below. (Queen Eleanor was the Queen Consort of King Edward I of England. When she died in the year 1290, the King is alleged to have had crosses built wherever her coffin rested on its journey down from Lincoln. This memorial is alleged to mark the last of these resting places.)

Of more technical interest is the fact that in the tunnelling for the Jubilee Line, and also in the Heathrow Piccadilly Line extension tunnelling, a laser beam was used to assist in setting out the tunnels and keeping tunnelling machines on course. It does not dispense with the theodolite procedure mentioned earlier, as there are tasks for which the laser is unsuitable. In brief, the apparatus directs a beam from a point in the rear of the workings on to a mark at the face, where it appears as a spot of light. It thus serves as a directional guide to the operators.

West of Charing Cross Underground station is a 30ft diameter track cross-over tunnel, whilst to the east along the line of the Strand the tunnels continue for ½km (3/10 mile) to a blanked-off end, located roughly beneath Lancaster Place just north of Waterloo Bridge. Described as over-run tunnels, they can be projected eastward if need be.

The tunnels for Stage I were driven mostly through blue clay. Because of the short intervals of drive, no 'mole' or similar digger was employed, the tunnel face cutting being done within the Greathead type of shield with pneumatic spades. Some 3km (1.86 miles) of the running tunnels were lined with ungrouted concrete segments, expanded against the tunnel walls, and keyed in near the base and the invert with wedge blocks.

The internal diameter of running tunnels thus lined is 3,810mm (12ft 6in), and 3,850mm (12ft 8in) where the lining is with cast-iron segments. Apart from Baker Street station, where the new station tunnel, lined with cast-iron, conforms in internal diameter with existing tunnels there (21ft 2½in), all other station tunnels have an internal diameter (in cast-iron) of 6,500mm (21ft 10in). The step-plate junction tunnels at their largest ends are 9,000mm (29ft 6in), to embrace both Bakerloo tube and new Jubilee Line tunnels.

South of Baker Street (that is, in tunnel) the track is laid on Jarrah wood sleepers, as is normal in tunnel furnishing. In general, the line has all the appurtenances of a new underground railway — too numerous to mention but including the big items such as ventilation shafts and new substations that have added to London's maze of subterranean works.

As to train operation, it was intended that the Jubilee Line *in toto* should be automatically operated, and Stage I south of Baker Street already incorporates the necessary features. Incidentally, the trains for the Jubileee Line are stabled and serviced at the Neasden Depot, which has meant displacing the Bakerloo trains from their erstwhile home there and building a new depot for them at Stonebridge Park. The short sections of by-passed track at each end of Baker Street station (adjacent to the step-plate junctions) are retained to provide a physical connection between the Jubilee and Bakerloo Lines and therefore a route for the latter's trains to Acton Overhaul Works.

The discontinued Stages II and III of the Jubilee Line would have offered fascinating studies. In it progress eastward across London via Fenchurch Street BR, its tubes would subsequently, due to the convolutions of the Thames, have been driven four times under the river in order to reach Woolwich and the new town of Thamesmead. Preparatory drillings along the line of route, on land and through the Thames river bed, are unlikely to be entirely wasted even though the Jubilee extension plans have been dropped in favour of a new project to serve part of East London; the Docklands Light Railway.

In 1981 a Government sponsored body called London Docklands Development Corporation (LDDC) was formed, to rejuvenate an area of about nine square miles within the Isle of Dogs. New industry and housing planned for this area of disused docks and wharves will need a form of rail transport, and the Docklands railway will meet that need, acting also as a link between the region and central London. There was such a rail link years ago but it was physically severed and service withdrawn before the last war. In 1984 the London Docklands Railway Bill received Royal Assent. It authorised the construction of a railway from the Minories (Tower Hill), through the London Docklands Enterprise Zone to the south end of the Isle of Dogs. Further Bills authorised the acquisition of lands for the construction of a north-south route of the railway from Poplar Docks to Stratford, and construction of an additional ticket hall at Tower Hill station.

As reported, Government will assist funding through a grant to the LDDC and a Transport Supplementary Grant. London Transport is acting as agent for the construction and operation of the railway, whose completion is scheduled as July 1987. The new Line's route will be along the BR Fenchurch Street-Southend viaduct as far as Stepney East. From there, it will run over part of the derelict route of the former London & Blackwall Railway into Poplar, where it will turn south, over the West India group of docks, to reach a terminal near Greenwich foot tunnel under the Thames. The north-south branch will use a disused BR freight line to Bow Road and then as a single track run along the existing BR line to a terminal beside the BR and Underground line to Stratford. The total route length is about 7½ miles (12.1km).

Brief details of the planned rolling stock and facilities are as follows: Unmanned stations on mostly elevated lines will have steps to platform levels, lifts for the disabled, closed circuit television and public address systems. Light transit trains, equipped for automatic operation and capable of negotiating tight curves and steep gradients, will be articulated twin-car units, which may ultimately run in pairs. Passengers will open train doors but operating staff on board will initiate train departure. Tickets will be obtained from automatic vending machines. Maximum system capacity is around 8,000 passengers an hour in each direction, although initial traffic will be very much less.

Mention of the old Blackwall Railway takes us back a long way. It was opened to Fenchurch Street in 1841 as a cable-operated railway, carrying

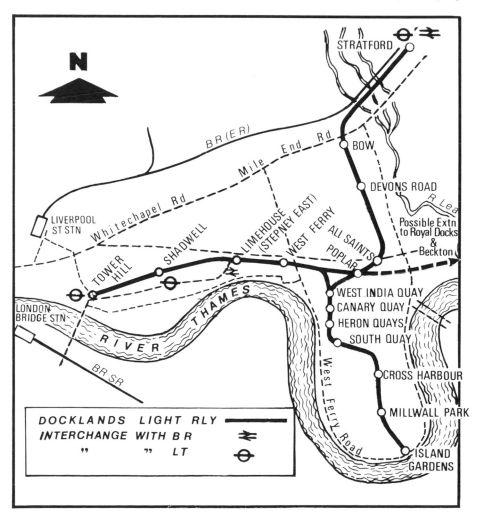

great numbers of steamer passengers from south-east coastal resorts, and from Gravesend, who landed at Brunswick Wharf, Blackwall; saving themselves 2½ miles by travelling to London by rail instead of making the longer river journey. Conversion to locomotive haulage took place in 1848; but other railways pushing into Essex and Kent took much of the Blackwall Railway's steamer traffic, and the development of Tilbury Docks eventually affected its local dock traffic. By the 1920s patronage was so down as to justify complete withdrawal of services.

A possible extension to the Docklands Railway would connect with the forthcoming Stolport (an airport for short take-off and landing aircraft), and serve the Beckton residential area. In 1871 a passenger railway extending due east for 1¾ miles from Albert Dock Junction (on the present BR North Woolwich line) was opened, to link London with Gallions on the Thames, where liners once called to disembark passengers. It was abandoned in 1950. The new railway would follow this old route to Gallions, the Stolport location.

The latest reports on the West India dock area indicate a growing financial interest in its development as an office centre. So much so that a consortium of foreign banks, having an option on a Canary Wharf site, is also exploring the feasibility of extending the dockland light railway underground from its Tower Hill terminus into the heart of the City. A Press report refers to existing tunnels which might accommodate the line extension.

Left:
The Docklands Light Railway is being built in part on the trackbed of the London and Blackwall Railway. This is the scene at West Ferry Road before work started. Note the hopeful 'STN' graffiti! *John Glover*

11
London Regional Transport

For some little time before 1 January 1948, the momentous first day of nationalised British Railways, labels bearing the new title, 'London Transport Executive' had appeared on certain London tramcars, and by the morning of 1 January the old order was extinct. The London Passenger Transport Board, a creation only 14½ years old, had ceded its vast system of public transport, including its railways, to the London Transport Executive of the British Transport Commission.

This was certainly a large-scale transfer, for the London Underground system alone then covered an area bounded by Aylesbury in the north and Morden in the south, in which nearly four thousand vehicles served over 239 miles of railway during the Board's last year; more than 554 million passenger journeys had originated on the London Passenger Transport Board system in that concluding twelve-month. As mentioned elsewhere, the Metropolitan Line was cut back to Amersham in 1961.

The Board had been in existence since July 1933 when it had assumed control to provide a co-ordinated transport system in the London area. The great Metropolis was fast outstripping what little railway extension had been carried out and it needed more surface transport, but before 1933 there was no single company prepared or able to put up the capital necessary for development schemes that were really urgent.

With the formation of the LPTB a new financial arrangement was arrived at, in the form of a committee incorporating members from the four main line railway companies and the Board. All receipts from any railways operating within the Board's special area were pooled, and after deducting expenses, the residue was allotted in proportion to the undertakings concerned. Thus the LPTB was allotted about two-thirds, the Southern Railway about one-fifth, and the remainder was divided between the GW, the LMS, and the LNE railways.

In 1935 agreement was reached between the Treasury and the LPTB, GWR and LNER whereby money was to be raised to enable these undertakings to embark upon an extensive improvement programme within the special area mentioned. The scheme covered conversion of steam-worked lines to electricity, and the extension of tube railways to link up with the lines so converted, work which has in part already been described.

Naturally, a great deal of money was needed, but the LPTB and the other sponsors were able to borrow it under terms attractive to the public, because the offered stock carried with it a Treasury guarantee. Thus the money spent on extensions, etc, did not come from the taxpayer's pocket, but from the investing public, whose interest on the loans was met out of railway revenue.

Since that time, London Transport has passed through a series of organisational changes. The London Transport Executive continued until abolition of the British Transport Commission at the end of 1962, when the London Transport Board was constituted as one of the four Boards, together with the Transport Holding Company, responsible to the Minister of Transport. Although co-ordination with the British Railways Board was to continue, there was a complete separation of the two organisations' finances.

Later in the 1960s, with growing staff shortages and industrial problems, and a deteriorating financial position, a new start was made. From 1 January 1970 under the Transport (London) Act 1969, the Greater London Council became the strategic transport authority for London. The Council appointed the members of a reconstituted London Transport Executive and made the major policy decisions. The rationale was to share the cost of running London's transport more equitably, and to link in with land use planning decisions. Government financial support for infrastructure projects was made available, and also for research and development.

The GLC period of control was terminated abruptly in the summer of 1984. With political control often opposed to that of the Government of the day, policy changes were all too frequent. Of lasting significance was the capital programme under which much new rolling stock was constructed, even if the later stages of the Jubilee Line construction and other system extensions recommended in the London Rail Study of 1974 were shelved. But the period will be chiefly remembered for the fluctuations in fares policies. At first, London Transport was expected to break even after depreciation expenses, to provide for any surplus which the GLC might determine, and to set aside a general reserve. This wholly unrealistic remit was gradually whittled down, and a fares relief grant was first made in 1974. The cost escalated alarmingly, and fares were doubled in eighteen months during 1975-76 to restore the position. Regular fares increases took place in subsequent years, but on 4 October 1981 the newly elected Labout Council reduced fares by 32% under their *Fares Fair* policy. Passenger traffic on the Underground increased by 7%, but the legality of the supplementary rate levied to finance it was challenged by the London Borough of Bromley. An appeal decision by the Law Lords ruled that the GLC's action was unlawful. Fares were raised by nearly 100% on 21 March 1982, and service economies were introduced later in the year.

Fares Fair saw the extension of a zonal fares system from the buses to the Underground system, and this was further developed in the next move, which reduced fares by one quarter from 22 May 1983. Travelcards, allowing

144

unlimited travel on Underground and buses within defined zones, were a runaway success. By the end of that year there were 600,000 holders of Travelcards, and passenger miles travelled on the Underground rose by no less than 20%. The number of passenger journeys made over these years reflected fares structures; in 1981, 1982, 1983 and 1984-5 respectively, these were, in millions, 541, 498, 563, and 659.

The Government decided that it could no longer countenance GLC control of London Transport, and under the London Regional Transport Act of 1984 the undertaking was transferred to the Secretary of State for Transport from 29 June. The duty of LRT is 'to provide or secure the provision of public passenger transport services for Greater London', and it must break even after grants. Early in the life of the new undertaking, objectives were set:

real fares to be held broadly stable beyond January 1985
no programme of major route closures on the Underground
improved interchanges and travelling environment
improved co-ordination with British Rail
the needs of disabled people to be given special attention
advice of the Passengers Committee to be carefully considered
unit costs reduced by at least 2½% each year for the next few years
revenue support reduced to £95 million cash in 1987-88.

In response, the annual Business Plan for 1985-86 set out the action it was intended to take. Overall Underground mileage would increase slightly, with the aim of maintaining the current high quality of service as reflected in passengers' lower average waiting times, down from 3.6 minutes in 1979 to 3.3 minutes in 1984. Investment in station modernisation would continue, with the target that by 1990 some improvement would have been made at more than 80% of stations since the programme began in 1981. Interchange improvements would continue, as would a number of measures to raise security for passengers and staff. Better publicity would include the publication of more local timetable books etc, while on stations the extension of centralised public address would be available at virtually all locations. More dot-matrix train indicators would also be installed.

One of the most significant of the Secretary of State's requirements was the reduction in unit costs, and reference has already been made to maintenance and the new ticketing system. Another major area concerns train operation, and it was determined that one person operation should proceed as quickly as possible.

The Hammersmith & City and the Circle Lines were converted to opo in 1984, using the C stock trains which were constructed with this in mind. District Line D stock is also easily modified, and all District services were to be so operated by the end of 1985. On the Metropolitan main line though, the A stock is of traditional construction with the guard's controls situated in the passenger saloons. An extensive conversion contract has been let for the 56 eight-car trains involved, and by autumn 1986 all will be equipped with train radio, public address system, headlights, dual controls for doors in the driving cabs, and new handbrakes.

Adequate driver observation of what is happening behind him is assured either by large mirrors or closed circuit TV monitors. Opo was not originally approved for tube lines (except for the automatically driven Victoria Line) by the Railway Inspectorate, due to concern at the possibility of a driver collapsing and causing a train to be stranded in a deep level tube tunnel. Recently a method has been proposed which uses radio to warn the line controller of a deadman's handle operation, and this may well form the basis of a system for tubes.

Automatic driving has certain advantages, mainly in respect of reducing delays at stations and providing a more consistent performance. This may justify the extra cost when signal renewal coincides with rolling stock replacement, but is unlikely to do so otherwise. There is a distinct tendency to driver boredom. Fully automatic train operation (FACT) is still being studied, but the problems of passenger safety in emergencies and staff surveillance have yet to be solved. Techically, the difficulties are few.

Although London Regional Transport remains the parent body, the Underground is now a separate business. From 1 April 1985, London Underground Ltd (LUL) becomes a wholly-owned subsidiary of LRT. The headquarters of both is in Westminster, occupying a huge office block through whose very foundations runs one of the busiest sections of railway on the system. The postal address of this building is modest enough — 55 Broadway, SW1H 0BD — and could mean as much to the complete stranger as a milliner's shop, for instance, yet he would find as he detrained at St James's Park station that above him towered a concrete structure housing many hundreds of staff, responsible for most things from a record of the date when Driver Smith entered the service to the estimated cost of the Terminal 4 project. The Broadway site was selected by the District Railway, towards the end of last century, though the present building dates from 1930.

In this building, and in other London Transport property dotted about London, are decided such diverse things as the purchase of 10,000 sleepers, or a batch of cars, or more uniform caps for stationmen. It is simply beyond the scope of this book to talk about any of these things, except that they are essential to the running of trains, but perhaps not quite so interesting to read.

There is still a lively interest in railways, both above and below ground. And that interest is likely to be maintained, so far as this book is concerned, in the increasing relationship between surface railways and those of the urban type, whereby the longer journey by surface rail tends to end in a shorter one by tube. For example, the 50 mile rail journey from Bedford by electrified services is often continued underground to London's West End through an interconnection at King's Cross. The trip from start to finish is thus under cover, and is an important consideration. An instance of the increased rail ridership this generates is illustrated by a review of the operation of British Rail's Inner Suburban services from Welwyn Garden City and Hertford North. The old London Transport tube from Moorgate to Finsbury Park was under-used because it came virtually to a dead end there. Since the suburban electrified services were projected through it, the tube carries 50% more passengers.

Not only in London but in other conurbations in this country and abroad, the underground urban railway network (rail rapid transit) has, or ideally would have, its inner stations spaced no more than ½-mile apart, so that the passenger's ultimate destination involves no more than a short walk. There may be two factors influencing a trend towards increased linkage and coverage of cities by rail rapid transit. The first is the need to relieve inner cities of some of the congestion caused by the motor vehicle — and the second, an awareness that the world's oil resources may be near exhaustion by the year 2000.

Conservation of oil is already an economic necessity in some countries and it could conceivably be a physical necessity, world-wide, in the future. However, railways of both varieties need not be dependent on oil, so that common sense dictates that they should continue to be viable; and viability should not be measured only in monetary terms. The immeasurable social and economic benefits they confer more than tips the balance in their favour.

For well over a century the Underground has been carrying passengers *en masse* in a frequent service of trains, and the future cannot alter this basically — only the surroundings will have changed.

Today there are few reminders of the past visible, and even these may vanish, or be demolished or hidden in the future. In March 1880 the first passenger-carrying steam train on the Metropolitan District Railway to Putney Bridge pulled into Fulham Broadway (then Walham Green) station. Today the station is little changed except for the electrified rails, and a steam train of the old vintage would not seem out of place there today.

Further back in time, Brunel's tunnel under the Thames was opened in 1843. Steam trains were projected through it in 1869. In 1884 the Metropolitan and District trains began to run through it at a time when the London Docks and Surrey Commercial Docks, which the line served, were figuratively bursting with ships, nearly half of which were tall-masted sailing ships.

Despite considerable changes, today's electric trains still rush down the slope of the old echoing tunnel after leaving Wapping, to its lowest point under the Thames river bed, and then climb the other slope on their way to Rotherhithe, Surrey Docks and the New Cross stations.

Such vestiges of London Underground's past are still to be found. Railway historians will probably go on seeking them out, if only to fill in the gaps which this book has unavoidably left unfilled, in the story of this unique and remarkable railway system.

Right:
1972 Mk I tube stock is seen at East Finchley closing its doors before departing southbound. Above is the Archer, by Eric Aumonier. *John Glover*

Below:
North Ealing station was built by the District Railway and opened in 1903. A 1973 stock Piccadilly Line train is seen arriving. *John Glover*

Appendices
1
Chronology of Principal Events on London's Underground Railways

Opening dates of sections of line until 30 June 1933

Metropolitan Railway

10 January 1863	Farringdon to Paddington
1 October 1863	Connection to Great Northern Railway at King's Cross
13 June 1864	Paddington to Hammersmith
23 December 1865	Farringdon to Moorgate
13 April 1868	Baker Street to Swiss Cottage
1 October 1868	Paddington to Gloucester Road
24 December 1868	Gloucester Road to South Kensington
1 February 1875	Moorgate to Liverpool Street, connecting with the Great Eastern Railway
12 July 1875	Moorgate to Liverpool Street (Met)
18 November 1876	Liverpool Street to Aldgate
30 June 1879	Swiss Cottage to West Hampstead
24 November 1879	West Hampstead to Willesden Green
2 August 1880	Willesden Green to Harrow-on-the-Hill
25 September 1882	Aldgate to Tower Hill
6 October 1884	Liverpool Street to Whitechapel
25 May 1885	Harrow-on-the-Hill to Pinner
1 September 1887	Pinner to Rickmansworth
8 July 1889	Rickmansworth to Chesham
1 September 1892	Chalfont and Latimer to Aylesbury (Old)
1 January 1894	Stoke Mandeville to Aylesbury
1 April 1894	Aylesbury to Verney Junction (absorbed)
1 December 1899	Quainton Road to Brill (absorbed)
4 July 1904	Harrow-on-the-Hill to Uxbridge
1 January 1905	Electrification, Baker Street to Uxbridge
1 July 1905	First stage of Inner Circle electrification inaugurated
2 November 1925	Moor Park and Rickmansworth to Watford
10 December 1932	Wembley Park to Stanmore

Metropolitan District Railway

1 October 1868	High Street Kensington to Gloucester Road
24 December 1868	Gloucester Road to Westminster
12 April 1869	Gloucester Road to West Brompton
30 May 1870	Westminster to Blackfriars
3 July 1871	Blackfriars to Mansion House and High Street Kensington to Earl's Court
9 September 1874	Earl's Court to Hammersmith
1 June 1877	Hammersmith to Richmond
1 July 1879	Turnham Green to Ealing Broadway
1 March 1880	West Brompton to Putney Bridge
1 May 1883	Acton Town to Hounslow Town
21 July 1884	Osterley to Hounslow West
6 October 1884	Mansion House to Whitechapel. Inner Circle completed and Junction made with East London Railway at Whitechapel
3 June 1889	Putney Bridge to Wimbledon
2 June 1902	Whitechapel to Upminster
23 June 1903	Ealing Common to Park Royal
28 June 1903	Park Royal to South Harrow
1 March 1910	South Harrow to Uxbridge
2 June 1932	Through working Barking to Upminster begun

East London Railway

1 October 1884	Underground services operated Whitechapel to New Cross and New Cross Gate until 3 December 1906
31 March 1913	Shoreditch to New Cross and New Cross Gate using electric traction

Great Northern & City Railway

14 February 1904	Finsbury Park to Moorgate

City & South London Railway

18 December 1890	King William Street to Stockwell
25 February 1900	Borough to Moorgate; closure of King William Street
3 June 1900	Stockwell to Clapham Common
17 November 1901	Moorgate to Angel
12 May 1907	Angel to Euston
20 April 1924	Moorgate to Euston reopened after reconstruction. Through running via Camden Town to Hampstead Line
1 December 1924	Moorgate to Clapham Common reopened
13 December 1926	Clapham Common to Morden, and through running via Kennington and Embankment to Hampstead Line

150

Waterloo & City Railway
8 August 1898	Waterloo and City, worked by London and South Western Railway

Central London Railway
30 July 1900	Shepherds Bush to Bank
14 May 1908	Shepherds Bush to Wood Lane
28 July 1912	Bank to Liverpool Street
3 August 1920	Wood Lane to Ealing Broadway

Baker Street & Waterloo Railway
10 March 1906	Baker Street to Lambeth North
5 August 1906	Lambeth North to Elephant and Castle
27 March 1907	Baker Street to Marylebone
15 June 1907	Marylebone to Edgware Road
1 December 1913	Edgware Road to Paddington
31 January 1915	Paddington to Kilburn Park
11 February 1915	Kilburn Park to Queen's Park
10 May 1915	Queen's Park to Willesden Junction
16 April 1917	Willesden Junction to Watford Junction

Great Northern, Piccadilly & Brompton Railway
15 December 1906	Hammersmith to Finsbury Park
30 November 1907	Holborn to Aldwych
4 July 1932	Hammersmith to South Harrow
19 September 1932	Finsbury Park to Arnos Grove
9 January 1933	Acton Town to Northfields
13 March 1933	Northfields to Hounslow West and Arnos Grove to Oakwood

Charing Cross, Euston & Hampstead Railway
22 June 1907	Charing Cross to Golders Green and Archway
6 April 1914	Charing Cross to Embankment
19 November 1923	Golders Green to Hendon Central
18 August 1924	Hendon Central to Edgware

Major events from 1 July 1933
1 July 1933	Formation of London Passenger Transport Board, under LPT Act 1933
31 July 1933	Opening, Oakwood to Cockfosters, Piccadilly Line
18 September 1933	Monument to Bank escalator link opened
25 September 1933	Opening of reconstructed Holborn station and closure of British Museum
23 October 1933	Opening, South Harrow to Uxbridge, Piccadilly Line

5 June 1935	New Works Programme, 1935-40 announced
1 December 1935	Quainton Road to Brill closed
6 July 1936	Aylesbury to Verney Junction closed
1 November 1937	All steam locomotives and goods rolling stock transferred to London and North Eastern Railway, except service stock
30 June 1938	1938 tube stock enters revenue earning service
31 October 1938	Opening of new Aldgate East station
4 December 1938	New Uxbridge station opened
3 July 1939	Opening, Archway to East Finchley, Northern Line
1 September 1939	Control of London Transport passed to Government through the Railway Executive Committee
20 November 1939	Opening, Baker Street to Stanmore, Bakerloo Line
14 April 1940	Opening, East Finchley to High Barnet, Northern Line
20 October 1940	Latimer Road to Kensington Olympia closed
19 January 1941	Opening of Highgate station, Northern Line
14 March 1941	Opening, Finchley Central to Mill Hill East, Northern Line
4 December 1946	Opening, Liverpool Street to Stratford, Central Line
5 May 1947	Opening, Stratford to Leytonstone, Central Line
30 June 1947	Opening, North Acton to Greenford, Central Line
23 November 1947	New White City station opened, replacing Wood Lane
14 December 1947	Opening, Leytonstone to Newbury Park and Woodford, Central Line
1 January 1948	Formation of London Transport Executive as a nationalised concern under the British Transport Commission, following Transport Act 1947. End of wartime controls
31 May 1948	Opening, Newbury Park to Hainault, Central Line
21 November 1948	Opening, Woodford to Hainault and Loughton, also Greenford to West Ruislip, Central Line
25 September 1949	Opening, Loughton to Epping, Central Line
18 November 1957	Opening, Epping to Ongar, Central Line
26 January 1958	First installation of programme machines for automatic junction signalling at Kennington
1 March 1959	Opening of interchange between Central and Metropolitan Lines at Notting Hill Gate
2 March 1959	Acton Town to South Acton closed
12 September 1960	Opening of electrification, Rickmansworth to Amersham and Chesham, Metropolitan Line
11 September 1961	Metropolitan Line services north of Amersham withdrawn; end of steam passenger working on Underground services
18 June 1962	Completion of four-tracking work, Harrow North

	Junction to Watford South Junction, Metropolitan Line
1 January 1963	Formation of London Transport Board, following Transport Act 1962
10 January 1963	Centenary of first Underground railway
5 January 1964	First automatic ticket barrier installed at Stamford Brook
5 April 1964	Full scale trials of automatic train operation commenced between Woodford and Hainault
4 October 1964	Finsbury Park to Drayton Park closed
10 October 1964	District Line services withdrawn between Acton Town and Hounslow West
5 February 1967	Opening of new Tower Hill station
1 September 1968	Opening, Walthamstow Central to Highbury and Islington, Victoria Line
1 December 1968	Opening, Highbury and Islington to Warren Street, Victoria Line
7 March 1969	Opening, Warren Street to Victoria, Victoria Line
1 January 1970	Formation of London Transport Executive under the control of the Greater London Council, following Transport (London) Act 1969
23 July 1971	Opening, Victoria to Brixton, Victoria Line
14 September 1972	Opening of Pimlico station, Victoria Line
28 February 1975	42 killed and 74 injured in tunnel end wall collision at Moorgate, Northern City Line
19 July 1975	Opening, Hounslow West to Hatton Cross, Piccadilly Line
7 September 1975	Services withdrawn Old Street to Moorgate, Northern City Line
5 October 1975	Services withdrawn Old Street to Drayton Park, Northern City Line
16 August 1976	British Rail commences services Old Street to Drayton Park
8 November 1976	British Rail commences services Old Street to Moorgate and Drayton Park to Finsbury Park BR station
16 October 1977	Opening, Hatton Cross to Heathrow Terminals 1, 2, 3, Piccadilly Line
1 May 1979	Opening, Baker Street to Charing Cross, and transfer of Baker Street to Stanmore branch to new Jubilee Line. Opening of interchange at rebuilt Charing Cross station.
28 March 1980	Opening of London Transport Museum, Covent Garden
4 October 1981	*Fares Fair* introduced by GLC, reducing fares by 32%

17 December 1981	Law Lords rule *Fares Fair* unlawful
21 March 1982	Fares increased by 96%
24 September 1982	Bakerloo Line services withdrawn Stonebridge Park to Watford Junction
22 May 1983	GLC reduces fares by 25%. Travelcards introduced
1 July 1983	Golden Jubilee of London Transport
4 June 1984	Bakerloo Line services restored between Stonebridge Park and Harrow and Wealdstone
29 June 1984	Formation of London Regional Transport under the control of the Secretary of State for Transport, following LRT Act 1984
1 April 1985	Formation of London Underground Ltd as subsidiary of LRT
Early 1986	Opening, Hatton Cross to Terminal 4 and Terminals 1, 2, 3, Piccadilly Line
July 1987	Opening of Docklands Light Railway, initial section

Notes

Dates shown as 'Openings' refer to the first day of public service. Thus although the Jubilee Line was officially opened on 30 April 1979 by HRH Prince Charles, public services south of Baker Street did not commence until the following day. Sometimes opening dates refer to the first Underground involvement. 14 April 1940 was the first day of electric traction from East Finchley to High Barnet, the Underground having supplanted the previous LNER steam service. Withdrawals refer to the first day on which the new arrangements applied; thus the last steam passenger services ran on 10 September 1961, and British Railways took over all services north of Amersham on 11 September. Throughout, present day names of stations have been used to avoid confusion; the station shown as opening on 25 September 1882 as Tower Hill, for instance, was originally named Tower of London.

Left:
One of the National Gallery paintings reproduced to decorate the modernised Bakerloo Line platforms at Charing Cross. This is a section from Rosseau's *Tropical Storm with a Tiger. LRT*

2
List of Underground Lines and Routes

	No of stations served	Route miles
Metropolitan:		
Aldgate to Amersham, branches to Chesham, Watford, Uxbridge; Hammersmith to Barking; Shoreditch to New Cross and New Cross Gate	69	58
District:		
Upminster to Ealing Broadway, branches to Richmond, Wimbledon, Edgware Road and Kensington (Olympia)	60	40
Circle:		
Mostly a combination of sections of Metropolitan and District Lines	27	13
Bakerloo:		
Elephant and Castle to Queen's Park, with peak hour extension to Harrow and Wealdstone	25	14
Central:		
Ealing Broadway and West Ruislip to Epping and Ongar, with a loop via Hainault	51	52
Jubilee:		
Stanmore to Charing Cross	17	14
Northern:		
Morden to Edgware and High Barnet via Charing Cross or Bank, with a branch to Mill Hill East	49	36
Piccadilly:		
Cockfosters to Heathrow terminal loop and Uxbridge, with a branch to Aldwych	52	45

Victoria:
Walthamstow Central to Brixton   16   14

Docklands:
Tower Hill (Minories) to Island Gardens, with a branch to   16   8
Stratford

Left:
A modern view of Great Portland Street station at street level. This building is a remodelling of the former Portland Road station, one of the schemes undertaken by the Metropolitan in the years around the first world war.
John Glover

Below:
Bayswater station has been altered little since its construction in 1868. Inside, the platforms retain their original elliptical iron and glass roof.
John Glover

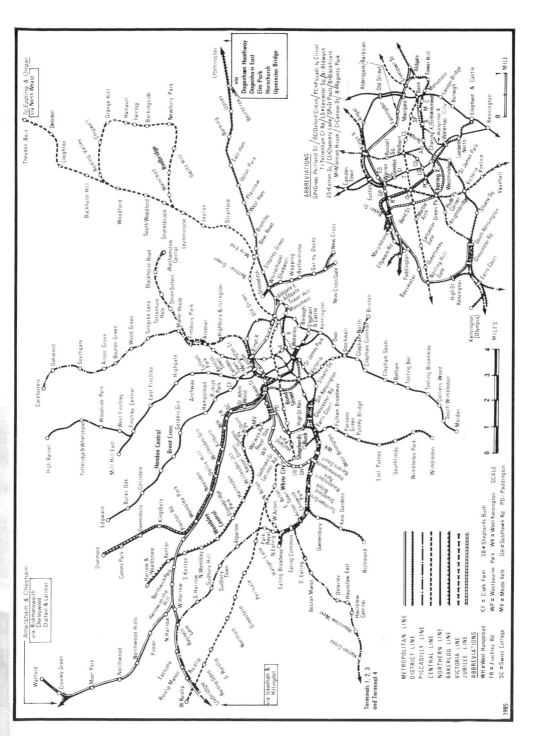

Index

Overleaf: John Glover

159

BAKER STREET

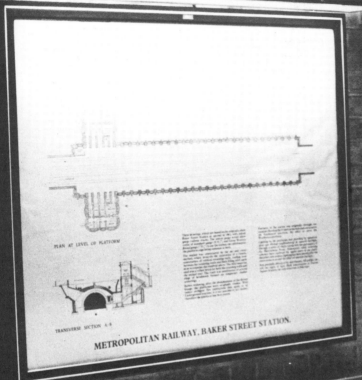

PLAN AT LEVEL OF PLATFORM

TRANSVERSE SECTION A-B

METROPOLITAN RAILWAY, BAKER STREET STATION.

BAKER STREET